TAKE THAT

AND

ROBBIE WILLIAMS

BACK FOR GOOD

TAKE THAT
AND
ROBBIE WILLIAMS
BACK FOR GOOD

EMILY HERBERT

JOHN BLAKE

Published by John Blake Publishing Ltd,
3 Bramber Court, 2 Bramber Road,
London W14 9PB, England

www.johnblakepublishing.co.uk

First published in paperback in 2010

ISBN: 9781843583264

British Library Cataloguing-in-Publication Data:

A catalogue record for this book is available from the British Library.

Design by www.envydesign.co.uk

Printed in Great Britain by CPI Bookmarque, Croydon CR0 4TD

3 5 7 9 10 8 6 4 2

Papers used by John Blake Publishing are natural, recyclable products
made from wood grown in sustainable forests. The manufacturing processes
conform to the environmental regulations of the country of origin.

Every attempt has been made to contact the relevant copyright-holders, but
some were unobtainable. We would be grateful if the
appropriate people could contact us.

CONTENTS

CHAPTER ONE

A REUNION MADE IN HEAVEN

On 15 July 2010, after years of speculation, the most popular boy band ever was about to re-form. Well, re-re-form, actually, as they had already done so as a highly successful foursome, but now it was truly going to happen. Take That was to be a five-piece again. Robbie Williams was coming home.

In truth, it had been in the pipeline for years. In the aftermath of his departure from Take That in 1995, Robbie had forged a stellar career, whereas the others hadn't. But in more recent years, Take That had staged one of the most successful comebacks the world of entertainment had ever seen, while Robbie's career hadn't glowed as brightly as once it had. At the same time, hostilities were largely over:

the rivalry between Robbie and his old bandmates, especially Gary Barlow, had cooled considerably. Indeed, they all looked set to be the best of friends once more.

As far back as December 2008, it had become clear that a reunion really was on the cards. Robbie was waxing positively lyrical about his old friends: 'The thing that struck me the most was how much fun they're having,' he said. 'It's more rewarding when you're a gang. Ever since I left Take That I've wanted to be in a band. We got together a lot over the summer. It was amazing. We've all matured a lot since we parted. I'm very pleased to say the differences we've had have just melted away. I celebrated by getting a Take That symbol tattooed on my right arm. I'm proud to know the boys and I'm proud to have been in the band. I'd love to be in the band again but I've got some unfinished business of my own.' And anyway – there were a few legalities to be ironed out first.

But still, a new tattoo of Take That's symbol? It must be serious. Gary clearly thought so, too: 'We will [reunite] one day,' he said. 'I just don't know when.' Although no dates had been announced, behind the scenes the wheels were being put in motion: Robbie's people were talking to Take That's people and all the interested parties were gradually edging back towards the fold. In March the following year, Robbie attended the opening of *We Will Rock You* in Manchester and came out for the idea more strongly still.

'I'm in regular contact with them, even Gary, and it's looking more likely by the week,' he observed. 'The lads all seem up for it and some people think it's a done deal. I think it would be fun. Let's see what happens, but my head's in the right place, so the timing could be right if Gary calls. I think it would be fun. It would be good. We've matured now. We'd have a laugh.'

In September 2009, the rumour mill went into overdrive. Robbie and the rest of the boys had reportedly been spotted in Electric Lady studios in New York. Was it possible that new material was on the cards? That had been one major sticking point last time around – that Gary was getting all the credit for songwriting (not least because he had written all the songs) and that Robbie hadn't been allowed to do his own thing. That issue clearly had to be addressed if the boys were to be together once more.

Robbie was 'back with Take That in the studio and they're all writing together again', said one source. 'Robbie wouldn't be happy performing old Take That songs that he has had no part in. But if they can pen new tracks that they're all happy with, they'll record them and he'll be back with them on stage.'

A spokesman for Take That, however, would not confirm that they were working on any new music and instead said the band was finishing work on *The Greatest Day*, their first live album, which was scheduled for release in November 2010. With neat timing, Robbie was also due to release a new album, *Reality Killed the Video Star*, the same month, but there was nothing like the potential rivalry there would have been had the two events coincided a couple of years earlier. Everyone was wishing one another well: it had become a veritable love-in.

There were rumours, although ultimately they came to nothing, that Robbie was interested in joining Take That on their spectacular 'The Circus Live' tour, which had been a knockout, both with the critics and with the ecstatic crowds. Finally, in November 2009, all five appeared on stage together for the first time in 14 years at a Children In Need concert at the Royal Albert Hall. They didn't actually perform together, however – they just embraced between numbers. The closest they came was when Robbie and Gary took to the mike together – with everyone else on the stage – for a rendition of 'Hey Jude'.

By this time, Gary was sounding every bit as enthusiastic as Robbie. 'It was lovely for us all to stand arm in arm and take a bow,' he said in an interview about the night. 'We've been in sort of real, proper contact for about a year now, and we've been hanging out and spending the evenings together. And when this night came up, I actually thought of Rob, and thought, "Wouldn't it be great if we could get him there?"' It had clearly been an emotional experience and there was more to come, with Gary saying they wanted to get back together and do something, but not just as a one-off. 'We want it to be a bit more substantial.'

Just how substantial was becoming increasingly clear. The following summer, in June 2010, the two were present at a charity football match for Soccer Aid at Old Trafford, England v Rest of the World, where they hugged in front of the wildly cheering crowds. Robbie was playing in the England team, alongside Ben Shephard, Bradley Walsh, Jamie Theakston, Ricky Hatton, Teddy Sheringham and Jamie Redknapp, while on the other side were Ryan Giggs, Zinedine Zidane, Woody Harrelson, Mike

Myers, Jens Lehmann, Gordon Ramsey, Shane Filan, Ronan Keating and Joe Calzaghe, with captain Michael Sheen. The match was a 2-2 draw, with the Rest of the World finally declared winners after a penalty shoot-out, but such was the intensity of the speculation surrounding a Take That reunion that the hug overshadowed everything else.

It seemed they had something to celebrate. Shortly after the match, it was announced that Robbie and Gary were to record a duet entitled 'Shame', which would be written jointly and would appear on Robbie's album *In and Out of Consciousness: The Greatest Hits 1990–2010*. That did, however, muddy the waters slightly for, although the two were evidently on excellent terms again, this was Robbie reunited only with Gary, not with the rest of Take That. Admittedly, the rivalry had been very much between the two of them but, briefly, the announcement deflected attention from the bigger picture. But not for long.

The release of the album was another indication that Robbie was looking back over the past and reviewing his life. Being a compilation, it encompassed his time with Take That as well as his solo career, and was bound to cause a period of reflection. All the boys were older now, closer to

40 than 30 (in the case of Howard and Jason, they actually were in their 40s), and if they wanted to sing together again, there was no time like the present. Time was moving fast.

Robbie clearly felt so. 'It's incredible to listen to the album and realise that it's already been twenty years of making music and playing gigs,' he said. 'And the great thing about the album is that it's not only a celebration of my past but also a bridge to the future. The fact that part of the future includes a name from my past makes it all the more poignant for me.'

There was disappointment in some quarters, however, that the other members of the band were not to be included. That soon evaporated when the announcement that everyone had been waiting for was finally made. On that hot day in July, a statement was put out: 'The rumours are true… Take That: the original lineup, have written and recorded a new album for release later this year. Following months of speculation, Gary Barlow, Howard Donald, Jason Orange, Mark Owen and Robbie Williams confirmed they have been recording a new studio album as a five-piece, which they will release in November.' That meant another single was on the cards, this one being 'The Flood'.

Everyone – not least the principal players in the drama – was absolutely delighted. 'I get embarrassingly excited when the five of us are in a room,' said Robbie bashfully. 'It feels like coming home.'

'Getting the five of us to be in a room together, although always a dream, never actually seemed like becoming a reality,' Mark chipped in. 'Now the reality of the five of us making a record together feels like a dream. It's been an absolute delight spending time with Rob again. But I'm still a better footballer.'

'I'm over the moon that Robbie's back with us, however long it lasts,' added Jason. 'I just want to enjoy our time with him. Life is beautifully strange sometimes.'

It wasn't long before they all got to work. They were all seen filming a promotional video, rowing on the Thames at Runnymede, Surrey, amid much merriment. 'They were having a great time – it was just five friends having a laugh,' said an observer at the scene. 'Robbie and the boys clearly got on very well. It was just like old times. They were mucking about and having fun. When they finished filming on the first day, Robbie decided he needed to cool off. He jumped straight into the lake and had a little swim. No one else had the guts to join him – it was freezing! The boys were stuck in a five-seater rowing boat wearing old-fashioned white rowing kits bearing a custom-designed Take That crest. They were told to paddle like the professionals. They were joined by a second boat with lookalikes and filmed pretending to race – only the band was being pulled by another vessel carrying the camera crew. I think they found it quite hard. If you haven't done it before, sculling can be pretty difficult. There were lots of little kids around and at one stage they all started singing "Angels" and Robbie was pretending to conduct them.'

All sorts of other outcomes were being predicted as a result of this reunion. Robbie famously suffered from stage fright but there was speculation that, once on stage with the rest of Take That, it would disappear. 'With the boys there the stage fright won't be an issue,' said a friend. 'I know he suffered from that earlier on. But he'll have all that support of his band of brothers. It's so wonderful that he has joined Take That again.'

Of course, despite all the lovey-dovey, no one was willing to take too much for granted. The original split, 15 years earlier, had been highly acrimonious and, for all the recent public hugging, Robbie and Gary had done their fair share of slagging each other off in the past. It was decided that the reunion would be for one year to begin with: that at least meant that there was an end in sight should the stresses of touring together prove too much. But there was real happiness surrounding the announcement as well. Robbie and his fellow band members did not just have an army of fans – they had a special place in the national psyche and there was real cheer that they would soon be working together again.

It was a welcome distraction from other issues that had been dogging the band, too. Take That had been one of the squeaky-cleanest outfits of their generation but, in the months leading up to the reunion with Robbie, they had been rocked by one revelation after another, suggesting that behind the scenes quite another story was playing out. It started with the cleanest living of the lot, Mark. In October 2009, he had married his long-term love Emma Ferguson, with whom he had two children: Elwood, three, and Willow Rose, one. In March 2010, the marriage was rocked by revelations that he had been unfaithful with at least ten different women, and that he had a drink problem. Worse, one affair, with Neva Hanley, had been going on for years, although Mark had not seen her since tying the knot.

There was nothing for it but to own up and

apologise, and Mark did. Indeed, no one was harsher on him than he was himself. 'I have been an idiot, a dick head, a knob head,' he said. 'All of the above and more. It's about me, my mistakes. Nobody else is to blame. I don't know how many girls there were in all. Maybe ten.'

Indeed, he sounded quite beside himself at times. 'I have been living with the guilt,' Mark continued. 'It has always been there – you carry it around with you. It held me back in my relationship with Emma. I wouldn't have done any of this if I had my time again. I am halfway through my life now and this, in a way, is a lesson. You've got to learn and that's what I am going to do. Emma is really strong and I know she will do what is right for her and the kids. I support that and I really appreciate that. She loved me – she still does love me – and I have let her down. That's the truth of it. You realise what you have done when you face up to it and the mistakes you have made. And I have really let her down. Friends, everybody. I feel like I have let everyone down. I wish I had told Emma about this before we got married and come clean then. I've done it now. It wouldn't be a second chance, it would be the hundredth chance she has given me.'

The last time Mark had seen Neva had been in

September 2009, before he'd got married, and it appeared to be something of a wake-up call. He had also provided Neva with some financial support and felt the need to explain that, too.

'When I met Neva in September, it was because I was having a tough time with Emma,' he said. 'I wasn't feeling very good about myself or the future and I went down my phonebook, found her number and we met up. After that last meeting I realised I had to try to sort my life out. I had to change the person I was. The wedding for me was a new slate and a new start. In my head, there was never a time when I was doubting getting married. It was a chance for me to put it all behind me and not make the mistakes I had made in the past.'

In some ways, Mark had been quite generous to Neva. She, alas, ended up feeling rather embittered about the whole affair (perhaps not surprisingly) but, whatever the rights and wrongs of the situation, Mark had helped her when she'd been in trouble. 'She phoned me the week before I got married,' he said. 'She said she had lost her job and was going to lose her flat, and asked if I could help her out. I have known her for years so I said, "Of course." In all I paid her about twelve k, the last one just last week. When I have been in a bad way, when I have needed a bit of support, she has been there for me. All the other girls were one-night stands. On tour. When I was away from home on wild nights out, which was every night. I'm not in contact with any of them. It wasn't the girls' fault, it was mine. I would be up for it and looking for it. I wasn't thinking straight. The next day I would think, "Oh fuck." It was regret – disappointment in myself. I had been drinking. I wouldn't have the nerve to talk to a girl when I'm not drunk.'

Increasingly, it became obvious that drink had played a big role in all this, and that Emma had had a fair amount to put up with. 'I denied to her I was having an affair when things were going on,' he said. 'It was getting better and better, me and Em. We met and, within a year and a half, she was pregnant with our first beautiful boy, Elwood. And when you have kids, things change. I feel like I am getting to know Em more and more every day. I love her to death but our relationship hasn't always been great, because of me. She has tried really hard to support me. Life was hard, I guess. I let Emma down. I was selfish and stubborn. Everything that has happened to me I have brought on myself. If ever we argued it was down to me.'

Since the wedding, however, there had been no

one else. 'I'm proud of that,' said Mark. 'I know that sounds really stupid but on our wedding day, for me the ring is really important and I want to be true to my word. It was a big change for me to be able to do that. It was a big moment for me, my wedding day. On many levels it was a fresh start and that was how I was looking at it. I have noticed a change since I stopped drinking, but I am quite difficult. It wasn't the sunshine Emma was hoping for but it is better. I have always liked a drink and I am a party man.'

Emma, not surprisingly, was livid, but the marriage survived, with Mark swearing it would never happen again. But it was still a terrible shock to the fans, who were used to thinking of Mark as the clean-living one, not a man with a drink problem who'd had a series of one-night stands. And just as the fans were reeling from those revelations, more stories started to come out.

It emerged that Howard had had an affair in 2008 with a married Dutch fan, 28-year-old mother of one, Merith van Onselen. Howard had been DJing in a club in Berlin at the time: he and Merith had had an eight-month fling while her husband Dave stayed at home and looked after the couple's three-year-old daughter. 'He has a very high sex drive,' said Merith, sounding utterly unrepentant. 'He wanted exciting sex and he sure got what he was looking for.'

Dave sounded less than thrilled. 'She was a fan,' he said sadly. 'Not many women would turn him down. She didn't.'

Could it get any worse? Yes. Now another Dutch woman came forward (although she insisted on remaining anonymous) to talk about an encounter with Gary who, she said, had taken her virginity when she was 17. 'The band Take That has a special sex manager who takes care of ladies for the band members,' she claimed. 'An interesting blonde woman made me find my way to Gary over and over again. The sex was very tender at first, but it didn't take long for him to show me what he had on offer. I was so naïve. The one time I came round without any help of the sex manager, I found him busy with another girl.'

And yet another Dutch woman had had a fling with Mark. 'Just like I was, Merith must have been mesmerised,' she said. 'We can't blame her for her actions.'

Indeed, Mark had been pretty busy. Yet more revelations came out, this time from an unnamed fan who said that Mark had persuaded her and a friend to have a threesome when they were just 16. The two were staying in the same hotel as him, which turned out to be very convenient indeed. 'He asked what we were doing,' the fan recalled. 'We said we were tired and about to go to bed. He said, "Want to come to a party in my room?" He told us to go up to the top floor in half an hour. It was clear that he was drunk. We walked into his room but there was no one in there, just the smell of incense. Because he was in Take That, I just thought they were trustworthy and nice. [But] he kept saying, "I want sex with you both," but I said I didn't want to. He even got condoms out of the bedside drawer.'

Activities ensued, although not, it would seem, full sex, and the girls returned for a second night. 'We felt obliged to please him,' said the fan. 'We did things to him and he did things to us. He kept on asking for sex, saying, "Come on, let's do it. It'll be safe." But we both refused.'

By this time, the revelations surrounding the band – especially Mark – were causing such ructions that they led to the postponement of the big reunion. Robbie's own domestic situation was still unsettled, on top of which the scandal would have totally overshadowed any announcement, so the plans were put on ice. 'All they care about is Mark at the moment and it wouldn't feel the same all of them practising for their comeback without him,' said a source. 'All excitement about the future is very much on hold because Mark's got to get better first.'

Several months on, of course, the reunion was announced, and a great deal of positive sentiment it evoked, too. However, with less than helpful timing, Neva Hanley finally went public with her side of the story about her affair with Mark. It didn't overshadow matters in the way it would have done had she spoken out earlier but it did serve to remind everyone that, behind the squeaky-clean image, there was another side to Take That.

Neva had, in fact, been in India since the scandal broke and only got back just as the reunion was announced. 'Great timing, isn't it?' she said. 'I spent months trying to get Mark out of my head. I come back and Take That are everywhere. I look at Mark in the papers and on the telly and he's this sweet, smiley boy and I find it really hard to equate that with the Mark I knew. I thought I loved him. I was very young. Now I feel used. He used to phone up and, like an idiot, I'd be there. I never demanded anything. I protected him. I lied for him. The one time I really needed him, he wasn't there. He couldn't care less.'

Neva had first met Mark when she was just 19,

at Preston station, and didn't have a clue who he was. 'I was heading home to Chester,' she recalled. 'This guy standing next to me said, "They take ages, don't they?" – they were prepping the train. He was small, smoking a cigarette and wearing a woolly cardigan.'

Perhaps the fact that Neva didn't recognise him until he was asked for an autograph was part of the appeal. 'He asked me to sit with him and paid for an upgrade as he was in first class,' she said. 'To be honest, I only vaguely recognised him from *Celebrity Big Brother*. He seemed like a nice guy. I had to get off at Crewe; he was going on to London. He scribbled his number down and said to keep in touch. I got off in such a rush, I didn't really thank him for the ticket so I texted him, then didn't think any more of it.'

Inevitably, Mark got in touch. 'I didn't recognise his voice,' said Neva. 'He said, "Hiya, it's Mark ... from the band." We spoke about football – he's a Liverpool fan and so am I. He started calling a couple of times a week. I didn't fancy him. I liked him. After a few weeks, he asked what I was doing at the weekend. I said, "Nothing." He said, "I'm in LA – come and visit me. I'll book you a room and pay for the flights." I would never do anything like that now but I thought,

"Why not?" I called the hotel to make sure he really had booked a room, then booked flights. I made sure they were flexible so that if I wanted to leave quickly I could.'

It was a little while before anything happened but when it did, it did. 'He just grabbed my arm, turned me round and kissed me,' said Neva. 'I was really shocked. I hadn't seen it coming. I think as you get older you get more attuned at picking up the signals but I really wasn't any good at that. Later, when we went out to dinner, he held my hand and I thought," OK, so I didn't just imagine that."'

The next day, the relationship was consummated. 'We started kissing and ended up sleeping together,' she said. 'It sounds awful, happening so soon. But for three days, we had spoken to nobody but each other. It felt right. It was very calm and easy. The only odd thing I remember was the next morning, Mark ordered tuna for breakfast.'

Unbeknown to her, Mark had already started seeing Emma but, even so, he invited Neva to his Lake District home. 'It was really beautiful, in the middle of nowhere,' she said, sounding rather wistful. 'There was a huge stone table in the dining room, which was all very dramatic. There were two kitchens, a study, a breakfast room, the blue room with his piano and spiral stairs to the main bedrooms. There was a huge copper bath in one bathroom and a wraparound shower in another. There was an orangery, which was freezing because it was November. I do remember thinking it was huge for just him, his two cats Coco and Basque and his pet crab. He'd had a tank full of fish but it had leaked when he was away in LA and only the crab had survived.'

To Neva, things all looked very promising. 'We talked for hours,' she said. 'There was a lot of kissing and touching. It was nice. I didn't really think about what our relationship was. We were friends but we had sex too.'

Although Neva was unaware of Mark's relationship with Emma, she was beginning to suspect. 'Another time, I'd had a rotten day temping and wanted to vent,' she said. 'I called Mark but he said he was in London and couldn't talk. Now I know that he was staying with Emma. If I'm honest, I had a feeling right then that there was someone else. There was a definite shift from that day on. He called only a couple of times a month and I only saw him now and then.'

In 2005, though, Neva moved to London and saw a bit of him then. For the first time, she began to realise that he might have a drink problem. 'It was about ten-thirty [in the evening] on the day I moved in,' she said. 'Mark called. He was very drunk. He said he was at the K West hotel [in West London] and wanted me there. I'd never seen him that drunk. He was needy. He wanted cuddles and kept asking if I liked him. I ordered him bread on room service and put him to bed. We didn't sleep together; he wasn't capable. The next day he was so sorry. That became the pattern of our relationship.'

In December 2005, now sure that Mark was seeing someone else, Neva received a round-robin text message announcing that Emma was pregnant. 'I wasn't even shocked,' she said. 'I just thought, "So she's called Emma." For some reason, I'd imagined her as Julie. The most upsetting thing was I'd been honest with him and he had this whole part of his life that he hadn't spoken about. I didn't respond to the text and we never, ever spoke about it.'

Life began to take off for Mark then. Take That had reformed and he was building his relationship with Emma – but he continued to see Neva from time to time. 'Mark craved attention,' said Neva. 'When he was on tour I could tell you the days he slept with other people. He would ring me, drunk, eight or nine times. When I said I wasn't going to him, he would go to the hotel bar and pick someone up. Every time he did that, he was taking a risk of being found out. I would worry when he called drunk. It's hard to break away from someone completely. I didn't see him that much then. He was too busy sleeping with the rest of the planet on tour. I saw him in October 2007, then January 2008, then nothing until a text in April.'

Finally, though, the cracks began to appear. 'Mark called me to tell me he was getting married,' said Neva flatly. 'I didn't react. I didn't love him particularly. I didn't want to sway him. It felt like there needed to be an end to it really.'

However, there was one more one-off. 'I regret that night completely,' said Neva. 'It was reckless in every way. Mark met me in front of the hotel, we went up to the balcony and stayed there drinking and smoking for five, six hours. Mark said Emma didn't like the person he was. I said she was probably stressed because she had two kids and a wedding to organise. He kept saying, "You like me, don't you, Neve?" He said I hadn't changed from the day we met and that he loved me. He was just drunk. But I had changed. I was five years older. Then he started talking about his stag do in New York. It was bizarre. We ended up having sex several times. I left before he woke up. I left a note telling him he should go home.'

Eventually, of course, it all came out, but Neva's attitude had hardened considerably by then. 'He made his choices,' she said. 'When everything came out, he just threw me to the lions. He didn't even call to see if I was OK. His manager wrote to make sure I was all right. Poor guy – sometimes I wonder how many other girls he had to write to over the years.'

Against all this, it was ironic that the reunion with the band's original bad boy, Robbie, diverted attention from all these antics. And it wasn't just the reunion that was capturing the public imagination. Just as his bandmates were having to put up with one shock revelation after another, Robbie, who had also had to deal with drink problems in his time, was at last settling down to find happiness with American actress Ayda Field. Indeed, he was so blissfully happy, he could hardly stop talking about it and, in August 2010, in the run-up to Take That's big reunion tour, he married her.

The proposal had been an unusual one: Robbie handed Ayda four cards, each bearing one of the words – Will. You. Marry. Me. 'Then he dropped on to one knee,' said Ayda. 'I said, "Yes."'

There was a reason behind Robbie's methods.

'When we first started going out, this weird thing would happen,' Robbie explained. 'When I had a deck of cards, I would split the pack and always come up with a Queen of Hearts. Because I'm into mysticism, it filled my heart and made me stop worrying about whether I was with the right person.'

The wedding took place at Robbie's home in LA. It was shrouded in great secrecy: guests thought they were being invited to a *Casino Royale*-themed party to celebrate Robbie's 20 years in show business, and had no idea they were about to witness his nuptials. It certainly wasn't your typical wedding: there was no best man and, rather than bridesmaids, the couple's eight dogs accompanied Ayda down the aisle. Nor was there any alcohol: the toasts were made with cups of Earl Grey. But it was a truly happy affair, with Ayda looking stunning in a Monique Lhuillier dress.

'Ayda looked like the most beautiful girl in the world,' said Robbie, who was clearly beside himself with joy. 'To be surrounded by family and friends and then see Ayda appear looking so radiant was almost too much to take. I'm the happiest man alive.'

And now, along with the Take That reunion, family life was on the cards. 'I'll probably have a couple and then adopt a couple, too,' said Robbie. 'I want one. Like Angelina's doing, I want one of them. Adopt two and have a couple. It's something we've talked about. When you go to somewhere like Haiti, it does make you feel like you want to help. I wanted to straight away – it's the instant guilt thing you get when you go out there. It's awful what has happened. Working with kids has made me want to have them. It's on the horizon. I don't know when. I've got a few things I want to do before that happens.'

One of those things was the Take That tour. The goodwill surrounding the band was as strong as it had ever been and their fans were now spanning generations. The original Take That devotees were now women in their 30s but who still adored the 5-piece, but they had also accumulated a whole new set of admirers who hadn't even been born when they first started out. So just who were these boys that generated such affection and loyalty? Where had they come from? How had it all begun?

CHAPTER TWO

IT'S A BOY!

The place was Burslem, a small town that forms part of Stoke-on-Trent. The date was 13 February 1974 and the locals at the Red Lion pub had something to celebrate. At the nearby Royal Infirmary, the pub's landlady, Jan Williams, had gone into labour with her second child. Her husband, Peter, was the pub's landlord.

'It's a boy!' the cry went up as Robert Peter Maximilian Williams made his way into the world, a half-brother to Sally, then eight, Jan's child from a previous relationship. Growing up in the pub, Robbie was an entertainer from the start, singing, dancing and showing off to the Red Lion's regulars. 'Rob used to come down after closing time in his pyjamas and would sing a song or do impressions,' his father recalled later. 'He would be doing Margaret Thatcher or Brian Clough. They loved it.'

Robbie showed a huge amount of drive from the outset, entering himself in a talent competition at the tender age of three. It was completely off his own bat. 'There was no pushy mother there, no parental supervision,' he said. 'My mum was actually shitting herself because she couldn't find me. It was just like, "There is the stage. I should be on that because I'm good at that."' He won.

But Robbie's early childhood was certainly not a blissful idyll. In fact, when he was little more than a toddler, events occurred that are widely believed to have contributed to the problems, specifically with drink, that plagued him later in life. A few months after Robbie was born, his father Peter won a pub comedy competition. The prize was £2. He then went on *New Faces* on television, for which he was paid £5. But these successes were to come at a very high price for, when Robbie was just two, his father decided to make a go of it professionally and launched a stage career under the name Pete Conway. He left the pub, went out on the road and shortly afterwards the marriage broke down.

Robbie always made light of this but the pain it caused him must have been considerable. 'Dad left when I was two,' he said matter-of-factly. 'We've become mates now but there's that blood link. My dad is very good at what he does. He's got excellent comic timing. He's so professional. That's what I admire him for. I was too young at the time to remember my parents' divorce. I can't wish for anything more than what I've got with my mum and sister; what I've got is fantastic. So I can't say I missed having a father full time. I mean, that's the way I grew up.' It was, but it is hard not to suspect that it also had its downside.

To a certain extent, Robbie's grandfather stepped into the breach, with a strong bond forming between man and boy. Robbie once recalled 'jumping up and down with my granddad, Jack Farrell, to strengthen me legs. He was in the army, a big man, Jack the Giant Killer, and he didn't want me growing up soft – so he'd get me to practise hitting him. I must have been three or four.'

Robbie, Jan and Sally, who he sometimes refers to as his second mother, were very close. Jan's mother Nan – real name Bertha – was also part of the family set-up, which was just as well as young Robbie needed a lot of control. He once threw the pub's

£3,000 takings out of the window on a Port Vale FC match day, followed by his mother's bra and his sister's knickers. It was a wild streak that would resurface some years on.

That urge to entertain was growing. When Robbie was four, he was taken on holiday to Torremolinos: halfway through the trip, he wandered off and lost his mother in the crowds. When she found him hours later, he was singing and dancing for the crowd – complete with busker's hat on the ground to collect loose change.

A teacher at Robbie's primary school, John Collis, cast Robbie in his first play – as the Devil. 'It was certainly suiting to his personality at the time and probably now as well,' Collis later recalled. 'I can still see him now with those little red horns on.'

Elements of the older Robbie were in evidence even when he was very young. A chubby little boy, Robbie would always have issues with his weight and once said that his earliest memory was of two little boys laughing at his belly on the beach at Babbacombe. But he was a popular boy. One of Jan's friends was Patricia McNair, a hairdresser, who had a young son, Jamie, with whom Robbie used to play. She also used to cut his hair. 'He used to come over on Saturday night and entertain us with his songs and dances,' she later recalled. 'Even then, when he was just seven, you could tell he was an entertainer. He was a great kid – naughty and lots of fun.'

Robbie was brought up a Catholic and that aspect of his life also endures. As an adult, he had a statue of St Teresa at the bottom of his bed when he lived in London's Notting Hill, a present from his mother. 'When I come home drunk, St Teresa turns her head away from me, I swear she does,' he once remarked. It was only partly a joke.

The first gig Robbie ever went to was by the pop group Showaddywaddy, who revived songs from the 1950s. 'It was fantastic,' Robbie recalled. 'I wanted the Teddy Boy outfit and everything but my mum wouldn't get me one because she thought I'd grow out of it. ' Robbie also made his mark on an international statesman early on. When Robbie was eight, Jan took him on holiday to the Victoria Falls Hotel in Zimbabwe, where they saw Joshua Nkomo, the country's president. 'I said to my mum, "That's the president of Africa,"' said Robbie. 'It was the time Lenny Henry was doing his African impressions and I went up to Joshua Nkomo when my mum wasn't looking, and I said,

"Hello, I'm Robert from England and I can do impressions of black men." And then I did my Lenny Henry. He just laughed and then I had a great chat with him. He was fascinated that a kid could just come up to him when he had men with guns – a kid who was not scared. He signed an autograph for me.'

Back home, however, there were problems on the business front. Takings at the pub were falling, so the family moved briefly to a council estate and then into a semi in the nearby town of Tunstall. Jan started running a florist's, while Robbie attended Mill Hill Primary School, taking part in school plays. He also joined a number of amateur-dramatics associations, including the Stoke-on-Trent Operatic Society, the Newcastle Amateur Dramatic Society and the Stoke-on-Trent Pantomime Society. By the age of 11, he was taking part in Hans Christian Andersen productions, playing the king's son in *The King and I* and the fiddler in *Fiddler on the Roof*. He was known as Swellhead, but also as Fatsikins because of his weight, by fellow pupils – he deflected this by making them laugh. His ambition back then was to become an actor – he hadn't even thought of being a pop star.

As Robbie entered his teens, he began to meet up

with his father Peter, who, before becoming a publican, had been a policeman and electricity inspector. The significance of this cannot be overestimated. It remains the most sensitive part of Robbie's life and one that, to this day, he doesn't like to talk about. But the fact is that throughout his early childhood, he hardly saw his father and this inevitably had an impact. When asked why he started bingeing on drink and drugs, Robbie once said, 'What do they expect me to say, that maybe my dad didn't love me enough?' It was a telling remark, as was the fact that the first time he got drunk was when he visited Peter in Scarborough, where he was working as a comedian.

'Rob is sensitive about Pete,' said Tony Hollins, Peter's best man and later his manager, 'because he doesn't want the public to know that there were a great many years when they simply weren't in contact at all.' When they did meet up, Robbie 'came to idolise his father', according to Hollins, but 'he realised that his mother had been left with the responsibility of looking after the family on her own'. Whatever happened subsequently between Robbie and his father, those were the formative years. It was bound to leave its mark.

But from his mid-teens, Robbie began to see his

father a lot more and was influenced by his taste in music – Frank Sinatra and Ella Fitzgerald. The two began to visit The Duke William pub in Hanley, where they would take to the stage in open-mic nights. 'He thinks he was just an average boy from Stoke but he was more talented than that,' said Peter. 'He always loved the stage. When he left school, he stood up in front of everyone and sang, "Every Time We Say Goodbye", the Cole Porter song. Robbie has sung that song since he was a kid and has recorded it himself. He grew up with Sinatra and Dean Martin and Nat King Cole because I was very much into them myself – still am!'

Robbie was also developing his own tastes. The first album he ever bought was Pink Floyd's *The Wall*. He also enjoyed Showaddywaddy, Adam and the Ants, Darts and lots of electronic music. He got his first taste of showbiz, at one remove, when Peter introduced him to a DJ friend: Robbie would help collate the sports news on a Saturday and sometimes do impressions during weekday afternoons, all for the princely sum of £10 a week.

By now Pete was dividing his time between the northern club circuit and summer holiday camps. Every summer, Robbie would spend three weeks with him at camps in Scarborough, Cornwall and

Wales, and started to learn the tricks of the trade. Robbie's stage persona has always been very cheeky chappy and this is where it comes from. 'I grew up on holiday camps,' he once said. 'I grew up with very old-school entertainers – their profession was to entertain people. Their expression, as they came on stage, was, "Always remember to smile." That was a sign on the door as you went up on stage: "Always remember to smile, 'cause they smile with you." Now it seems that there's a sign on the door saying, "Always look at your feet, because if you look at the crowd, you might get scared and you might scare them, too."' That certainly wasn't a philosophy that young Robbie ever practised.

Robbie moved on to St Margaret Ward RC High School, where he became the class clown and became very interested in football. Academic work did not feature highly. As an adult he has voiced regrets about not working harder at school but, at the time, his interests were football, acting and girls. Little Fatsikins showed early signs of becoming a ladies' man: he lost his virginity at 14. 'She was tall, red-haired and mad for it,' he later recalled. 'She came up to me in classroom one day and, in front of my mates, said, "Your place, Friday, after school." Of course, I put on a big, macho show as if to say, "Of course, I've done this dozens of times." But although I fancied her, this girl scared the life out of me. On the Friday, I took her home and, after a quick snog, completely lost my bottle. But as I asked her to leave, I suddenly realised how much stick I was going to get from my friends. I took her up to my room and about two and a half minutes later, it was all over. It was a less than impressive performance but I was thrilled and naturally told all my friends what a stud I'd been.'

At the age of 15, Robbie landed the role of the Artful Dodger in the North Staffordshire Amateur Dramatic Society's production of *Oliver!* – a part that was to prove something of a watershed in his life. Brian Rawlins, who was the founder of the society and played Fagin, remembered young Robbie fondly. 'When we were rehearsing, we got a professional pickpocket to show us how it should be done,' he said. 'Robbie became very good at it. You would keep finding things missing in rehearsals and then Robbie would pop up waving your wallet, or whatever he had taken.

'Robbie was a nice lad with lots of personality and confident even then. He was very much the local boy, with a strong local accent, which he had to cover up when he played Dodger. His mum was great, too – they were very close. He helped every Saturday afternoon in the flower shop she owned in Newcastle-under-Lyme. He was a bright lad, with a spark in his eye which still comes across now, but he was also very sensitive. He would get upset if he was ever told off and would get quite emotional about it.'

It is fair to say that playing the Artful Dodger changed Robbie's life. 'It was my first lead role,' he said. 'And I walked out from the side of the stage, whistling and doing this walk, and the whole audience just took a breath, gasped. I physically heard them do it. I'd just won them over by walking on stage. And I can always remember coming out for the curtain call and my cheers drowning everyone else's out. I thought, "I am really good at this."' He was right.

That year was to be a turning point in many ways, carrying with it upheaval and sadness, as well as opportunities. Robbie's much-loved aunt Jo, his mother's sister, died, bringing a great deal of anguish to the family. Some months later, Robbie's mother Jan turned on the radio and heard an entrepreneur called Nigel Martin-Smith talking about founding a new boy band, one to rival the massively popular New Kids on the Block. Pretending to be Robbie,

Jan wrote in and asked for an audition. Robbie got his audition but Nigel was unconvinced; Jan sent in copies of local press cuttings talking about Robbie's 'uncanny stage presence'. The wheels had begun to turn.

Robbie sat his GCSEs and, to no one's surprise, failed the lot. He wasn't thick but he'd done no work, on top of which he'd taken acid for the first time just before his RE exam. Even so, it was a blow when he learned of his grades. 'Me and my friend Lee just got our exam results and we both failed really badly,' he later recalled. 'We didn't know how we were going to tell our parents. So we went to the bottle shop and bought ten each of the cheapest cans of bitter we could buy and sat on the bowling green and just necked these bitters – trying to figure out a way to tell our parents because they had hoped for so much for us. They wanted me to go on to university. I went back to my mum, pissed, and said that I had something to tell her and she said she had something to tell me – "You're in the band." Then she said, "What did you have to tell me?" and I said it didn't matter. I ran upstairs and shouted at the top of my voice, "I'm going to be famous!"' As one door had shut, another had opened. Robbie was on his way.

Ironically, given the band's later incarnation, Robbie's inclusion was an afterthought. Martin-Smith had originally wanted a foursome and had already got it. Gary Barlow, the singer/songwriter, Mark Owen, the looker, and Jason Orange and Howard Donald, the dancers, were already on board. Then, early in 1990, he received Jan's letter. 'I originally wanted Take That to be a four-piece band,' he said in later years. 'The only reason I took on a fifth was because I thought one of them would be bound to drop out, get a job at Tescos or get married.'

Like Robbie, Martin-Smith had left school at 15 with no qualifications. In 1981, he'd launched a modelling agency, which went on to employ ten staff and make a £1 million annual turnover. But he wanted to manage a pop group: 'I'll just trust my instincts,' he said of the way he put the band together. 'They need no singing skills, but they must be able to move well and have star quality. Yes, that's vital.' The band's name was inspired by Madonna, who'd grabbed her crotch in one performance and shouted, 'Take that!'

At first there was some debate in Robbie's family as to whether he should join the band. It was originally formed to appeal to the gay circuit – Martin-Smith is gay – and was set to perform in gay clubs. 'I didn't know that sort of thing happened,' Robbie said. In later years, there has been a great deal of speculation about Robbie's own sexuality, a lot of it fuelled by him. The reality is almost certainly that, while still a young man, he was introduced to a world he had never seen before and – half-joking, half-fascinated – made a few remarks that were later open to question. As his marriage later proved, Robbie is totally straight. Even so, his family were a little worried: was this quite the right milieu for a young and impressionable boy? His father Pete was relaxed, pointing out that the world of show business is full of gay men, and Robbie's grandmother took an even more robust point of view. 'I'd be more worried if he was going to become a priest,' she said.

And what did the four young men of Take That think? They'd been all set to go as a quartet when they suddenly discovered they were about to have a new boy in their midst. 'This picture looked like a fourteen-year-old school kid,' said Gary. He was only one year out. 'The manager said, "His name's Robbie and he's got a really good voice." He was one of those precocious school kids, who danced outrageously and was dead cheeky but quite a likeable young lad.'

Martin-Smith, meanwhile, was delighted with his discovery and, despite the later bitterness between them, spoke warmly of his young protégé in the early days. 'Robbie Williams is a huge talent, but his talent is not just for music,' he said some years after the band was formed. 'It's for playing the part of being a rock star. When he auditioned for me, he did impressions – and very good ones. I remember in the very early days of Take That, we were in a karaoke bar and Robbie got up and sang "Mack the Knife". He could have been Frank Sinatra. He was amazing. I knew he had bags of talent. He only gave away a bit at a time.'

And so in September 1990, the contracts were signed. It was much like starting a new school term: so much lay ahead and they were all young and nervous. 'I remember the first time I ever met the lads at the Take That auditions,' Robbie later recalled. 'I came with my mum and I was saying out of the corner of my mouth, "Right, Mum – go now." Marky was doing exactly the same thing at the other end of the street with his mum. As I walked into the audition, there was this guy sat there with really untrendy Adidas bottoms on, massive Converse trainers, a stupid, spiky haircut – and I'm not dissing him here. I mean it lovingly.

He's got his legs crossed, with his hands on his knee and this bloody leather briefcase, which had song sheets for crap cabaret songs in it. I looked at him and I was told, "This is Gary Barlow. He's a professional club singer and he's going to make this group happen."

'Then there was this guy called Jason, who was all full of himself because he'd been on *The Hit Man and Her* and I was completely impressed. The fact that Jason had been on telly and liked RS2000 cars made him God in my eyes. He was cocky and strutty and I just thought he was great. Then, as I was halfway through my audition, in walks this other bloke called Howard – who was late as always. And he was really shy. So that was the scenario. Take That met for the first time and I remember just looking round and thinking, "Oh shit! I wish I'd passed my exams!"

'Then Gary called me over and said, "Right, son, here's what you do." He called me "son"! He made me laugh from that moment on. He's got this brilliant northern humour and it's all really clever, quick one-liners. He's got loads of jokes – he is Gary "Bernard Manning/Roy Chubby Brown" Barlow. Me and him used to have some laughs.'

And so rehearsals began. Robbie commuted

between Manchester and Stoke-on-Trent (Jan paid the £8 fare) as Take That worked with a producer called Ian Levine. It took Robbie a while to settle in to his new life: he felt trapped and resentful. Indeed, he nearly left until his father talked him round. 'I walked out of rehearsal one day and went to see my dad,' Robbie said. 'He was a bluecoat, working the holiday camps. I wanted to go on the road with him and leave the band but he gave me a sobering lecture. He told me toilet rolls don't grow on trees, you have to buy them, you have to learn to do your laundry and iron, you have to buy food and cook for yourself. He made me realise what a tough life it could be when you don't earn much money and then he said to me, "How are you going to feel when they are at No 1?" So I put my head down and stayed.'

Robbie was later to claim that the band's management had deliberately favoured Gary rather than him, but the fact was that Gary was seen as the pivotal member of the band and Robbie was not. Nor was he working as hard as the others wanted him to. 'Rob didn't want to learn the routine, or else he was the slowest,' said Kim Gavin, the boys' choreographer. 'Everyone else would get up and go and have a break, and you'd have to go over it with him quite a few times. He'd make a joke of it, of course, but he was the last to learn.'

The band's first gig was in a nightclub in Huddersfield called Flicks and it did not herald future glories. 'There were only about twenty people out there and a dog, and only about ten of those were interested in watching,' Gary said. They got £20 each – which, as Jason vividly put it, 'paid for a Kentucky Fried Chicken for each of us'.

Then the sessions in gay clubs began, rather better paid at £500 a time. 'At the beginning, our following was totally gay,' Robbie said. 'Totally gay. At the start, we did gay clubs and that. And it was fucking good groundwork for us. The gay clubs and the gay community – they embraced us with open arms. I think that anything the gay community comes up with will be dissed at first. Dismiss the music, dismiss the clothes, dismiss everything 'cause it's gay. And then, like, two to five years later, everyone's going, "Fucking hell! I'm mad for that music! I'm mad for those clothes!" And it's always the same. The gay community embraced us with open arms and then, before you know it, "Fucking hell, Take That, yeah! I've always quite liked them." I suppose that was my first taste of fame. The first time I was totally approved of.'

There were a lot of firsts going on. Robbie started experimenting with drugs, mainly ecstasy. They were going through their leather phase: legend has it that they were walking past London's Hyper Hyper on Kensington High Street when Jason saw a leather jacket with tassels, bought it and then everyone else wanted one. Nigel Martin-Smith started circulating demo tapes and got them a spot on Sky TV: they performed two numbers and were interviewed for ten minutes. Fame remained aloof.

Nigel was pretty sure of his band, though, so he remortgaged his house and used the funds to release Take That's first single, 'Do What U Like' on his own label, Dance UK. It only charted at UK No 82, and the accompanying video made it pretty clear where they'd spent the last year. Although there were a few girls present, they were all dressed in black leather, writhing around naked on the floor and covering each other with jelly. It was banned from primetime television but it was enough to get some interest going in the industry. In September 1991, exactly a year after they'd started, the boys landed a deal with RCA.

On signing the contract, each of them got a £20,000 advance, although the deal didn't always bring what they'd expected. 'We were all in B&Bs,'

said Gary much later on. 'We'd get to our room and open the door and there'd be five single beds. I'd never had friends quite like these before. I hadn't been used to making sacrifices. I was quite a bold, selfish person at that time. And there was a bit of snobbery as well, because I was the musical one, at the end of the day. But I grew to love these four people I was with.'

A month later, Take That's second single, 'Promises', was released. By now the band was starting to reach out to teenage girls rather than gay men, so the leather was banished and the boys toured the country, putting in appearances everywhere, including *Wogan*, *Pebble Mill* and *Going Live*. 'Promises' entered the charts at UK No 38.

But the expected lift-off didn't happen. The earlier strategy of playing gay clubs might have taught them their trade but it hadn't established the mainstream following they needed now. Their third single, 'Once You've Tasted Love', only made it to UK No 44 despite, rather bizarrely, the boys touring with the Family Planning Association to promote awareness of safe sex. 'We're becoming the most famous people in Britain for not having a hit,' Gary snapped.

Other people were beginning to wonder, too. 'We

had been giving them a lot of space and, after their second single with RCA bombed, we wondered if we were flogging a dead horse,' said Mike Soutar, then editor of *Smash Hits* magazine. 'Other bands would have given up. They set out to find fame and fortune or whatever, find what they are looking for and don't like it. Take That are talented and resilient and have what it takes. The key to their success is that they are very hardworking, are genuine good blokes and they are believable.'

And so they knuckled down. The release of the first album was postponed and the band went all out to nurture the fan base they needed, performing four shows a day. There would be a school gig during the day as part of the 'Big Schools' tour, an evening matinee, an under-18s club and an over-18s club. Slowly it began to pay off.

'When we were first signed up by RCA, we did think we were going to make it right away,' said Gary. 'We didn't and we learned a lesson. We went round all the clubs, everywhere from schools, youth clubs, gay clubs – we covered the lot. We worked at the grassroots level because that's where it really counts. Fans don't just appear out of thin air. You have to make people like you – you have to give them something. By the time we released "It Only Takes A

Minute", people from Doncaster to Devon and Dundee actually knew us from appearances on their doorstep. Then, all of a sudden, it took off.'

But it wasn't much fun at the time. Radio 1 declined to play 'Once You've Tasted Love', which badly knocked its chances of success and their confidence, too. Robbie, now 17, was considering leaving again. But Gary, above all, was determined that they should fight on.

The turning point came with a show at the Hollywood disco in Romford, Essex. They had invited the pop editors of three newspapers but the only one that turned up was the *Daily Star*'s Rave team, who met the boys for a drink and were then driven on to the gig in the band's 'That-mobile' – actually a mini-bus. They were particularly taken with Robbie, who entertained them with 'impressions of Norman Wisdom and Bros', before becoming even more impressed when they saw the show. Rave invited them to play at a Christmas party in London's Limelight Club in front of 'dozens of VIPs', where they met some of the movers and shakers in the music industry. This time round, at long last, everything fell into place. After slogging around some of the most basic gigs in the country, learning their trade and building up a fan base, to say nothing of battling disappointment and setbacks, Take That were about to become the hottest ticket in town.

CHAPTER THREE

TAKE THAT
TAKES OFF

'I've had to change my telephone number a couple of times,' said Robbie. 'A few of the fans who work as operators found my number. Also, a few fans' dads are policemen and they've been giving the girls my number. If I found out who it was, they'd be in serious trouble!'

The year was 1993 and Take That were at the height of their fame. There was no more touring school assembly halls, no more gay clubs and no more trying to convince the record industry that they had what it takes – the boys were on top of the world. Still not yet 20, Robbie and the band had toured the world, notched up four hit singles and proved to the world that they had what it takes. But fame was taking its toll. Robbie's grandmother had

had to sell her house after it, too, was constantly besieged by fans.

The boys were living pretty much on top of each other and, with hindsight, it's easy to see that tensions were beginning to emerge. In an interview with *TV Hits*, given when he was just 19, Robbie was asked if Gary had written most of the tracks for their second album, *Everything Changes*. 'Yeah, he's written all the stuff,' he replied. 'He's loaded – I'm a pauper next to him! No, he wrote all the stuff, which we're happy about because it gives the band added credibility when you write your own stuff. I've actually just been listening to it and I'm so excited about the next album, more so than the last one, really.

'I know it sounds sick but we do spend a lot of time together and we enjoy every minute of it. We live in each other's pockets twenty-four hours a day, seven days a week and we always manage to have a laugh. Even if we're having an argument, we always make a laugh out of the argument! It's a pleasure being with the guys... They're a bunch of idiots, though. Except Mark!'

Behind the scenes, it was a little different. Nigel Martin-Smith had imposed a very strict regime of no drink, no drugs and no girlfriends, and it was beginning to grate. The boys were pop stars, after all, with constant temptations in front of them and, given that Robbie had been drinking since he was 13, he was finding it difficult to do as he was told. Towards the end of 1992, he sparked a craze for sucking rubber dummies, until someone made the connection that ecstasy users suck dummies because the drug makes them want to chew. 'Please don't fret, I am not on drugs,' said Robbie hastily, as letters poured in from fans begging him to get help, but he was later to confess that he'd loved taking ecstasy. The clues were there if you knew where to look.

To the outside world, however, Take That were having the time of their lives. In November 1992, with 3 Top 20 singles behind them – 'It Only Takes A Minute', 'I Found Heaven' and 'A Million Love Songs' – the boys set off on their first tour as fully fledged pop stars. They started in Newcastle City Hall in front of a 2,000-strong audience, 6 of them men, with the excited girls screaming at their new heartthrobs. The presence of those men, however, reminded everyone that Take That's past was not as innocent as its present. 'We are happy to perform at gay clubs,' said Jason. 'I'm really proud of our gay following. We get a lot of fan letters from men and I love reading them.' Robbie added, 'It's very flattering that both sexes fancy us.'

The boys were pretty clear about their own sexual preferences, however, and inevitably they were the targets of very willing groupies. Nigel was not amused but the boys were thoroughly enjoying themselves. Robbie remembered his first such encounter: 'Take That hadn't been long together when we did a show on the Isle of Wight,' he recalled. 'Later we did an official meet and greet with some local girls. One was an absolute stunner. She was older than the rest, about twenty, and while we were all posing for a picture with the girls in front of us, she reached behind her and grabbed me in the most sensitive region. The photographer was snapping away and I was having the time of my life. I think I made him take about eight rolls of film.

'It suddenly struck me that she was a groupie – someone who liked sleeping with pop stars. Afterwards, I told her to visit my hotel and gave her my room number. When we arrived back, she was waiting for me outside the hotel. Nigel spotted her and ordered me back to bed. I went to my room and Mark came in to console me but suddenly there was a knock at the window. I peeped behind the curtains and the girl was standing there, topless. She hadn't spotted Mark, so I told him to hide in the wardrobe so he couldn't run off and tell Nigel. As I tried to pull her in through the window, she screamed and woke Nigel in the room next door. He burst in to find this half-dressed lass stuck in the window, Mark laughing his head off and me still desperate to get my hands on my first groupie. He wasn't happy, to say the least. Mark was sent back to his room, the girl was sent packing and I had to have a cold shower.'

It might not have worked that time but it certainly did from then on. The boys, all five of them, were constantly propositioned and often managed to take up the offers. Robbie recounted numerous other exploits, including one occasion in Monte Carlo when he had returned late to his hotel with the room number of one ardent fan, who was sleeping only a couple of doors away. Robbie couldn't walk down the corridor in case the band's security men saw him, so instead he climbed, drunk and naked, across the intervening balconies to get to her room. He made it but he was lucky – one slip could have ended in a long drop to the sea.

The boys' stage act certainly encouraged such antics. They would regularly strip on stage – although never completely – and ended their numbers by turning their backs to the fans, whipping down their trousers and revealing TA KE * TH AT across five pairs of buttocks. Girls would camp outside their hotels chanting, 'I want to see you naked,' and were driven to further fervours with the January 1993 single, 'Why Can't I Wake Up With You?' The band won seven trophies at the *Smash Hits* awards evening and spent a fortnight in Manhattan, plotting to break America, although Robbie and Mark complained that they wouldn't be allowed into US clubs as they were not yet 21.

Take That toured Japan and Europe and there was talk of a movie (it never came off), and in 1993, they received 57,000 Valentine's cards. Money was beginning to come in but, with the exception of Gary, who bought himself a £60,000 house, the rest of the band was still on a tight rein, living on an allowance of £150 a week. The record company provided food and clothing but Robbie, Mark and Howard were all still living at home.

The pressures of fame were beginning to tell, though. The boys could not go out in public to do ordinary things such as shopping or going to the pub any more – they would be mobbed and have no privacy whatsoever. Being together all the time could prove claustrophobic and some of the eccentricities Robbie displayed later were becoming public: a belief in ghosts, for example, which was so real and so genuine it would keep him awake at night.

But the Take That juggernaut thundered on. Their next single, 'Pray', shot to UK No 1, while the tour continued. When it reached Manchester, home to all the boys except Robbie, hysteria rose to levels that hadn't been seen before. When the band turned up for a photo session at Manchester United, they got trapped inside a police van by frenzied admirers; minders had to form a human corridor for the boys to be able to make their way into Old Trafford.

Although it was Gary who was the lead singer, Robbie continued to show a propensity to grab the limelight. The boys played Manchester's G-Mex Centre: 'Take the roof off!' cried Robbie and the fans complied. The boys then announced they would be donating the proceeds of the concert to United skipper Bryan Robson's £1.5 million appeal to buy cancer-detecting equipment for the Royal Manchester Children's Hospital. All were generous; Robbie had paid his Nan's gas bill from his first pay packet.

Each member of the band has his own persona. Mark was the heartthrob, while Robbie was the clown. By the end of 1993, they were riding higher than ever: they swept the boards for the second time at the *Smash Hits* awards, with the Best Group, Best Album and Best Pop Video trophies; Mark won Most Fanciable Male Star and Best Dressed Person; Jason got Best Dancer in Pop and a newly shorn Robbie achieved Best Haircut. 'Babe', their third UK No 1, got to the top of the charts in time for Christmas. It seemed they could do no wrong.

By early 1994, however, there were rumours that one member wanted to leave the band – Gary. He was very much seen as the force behind it all, the talented one, the songwriter, while the others were, how to put it, a little expendable. Even the likes of Sir Elton John were singing Gary's praise, while the man himself was talking about relocating to Los Angeles. But the group was doing so well – in April, their next single, 'Everything Changes', went to UK No 1 – that he decided to stay.

In fact, 'Everything Changes' became their fourth consecutive single to enter the charts at UK No 1, making musical history. A tribute band, Fake That, appeared and, such was Take That's popularity, Fake That started to be courted by the music industry. Even association at one remove was a draw.

But the boys were being driven really hard now.

Aware that their shelf life was limited (no one could have foreseen that they would still be going strong 20 years after they were founded), record industry bosses were getting them to do so much that cracks were beginning to appear. They nearly refused to go on stage just before one show at Wembley because they were all so tired, while Jason presciently warned that Robbie was in danger of going off the rails because he'd missed so many of his teenage years.

It was a trial for other reasons, too. Robbie was still living at home, which meant that his mother Jan's house was all but under siege, surrounded by fans day and night. At Christmas 1994, matters came to a head: 40 fans set up camp around the 1930s 3-bedroom semi on Greenbank Road, Tunstall. It was too much. Robbie himself appeared at the door to ask them to go away and got a very hostile response as a result.

'I've travelled nine hundred kilometres and waited four hours just to be snubbed,' complained Natalie Gansauge, 20, from Dortmund.

'I forgive him for being arrogant,' said 16-year-old Rebecca Barton, from Chelmsley, Birmingham. 'To see his bum was worth waiting for.'

Other fans started painting messages to him on nearby properties. Jan had had enough. She put the property up for sale at £57,950, which meant that local estate agents were promptly flooded with enquiries, not from potential buyers, but from Robbie fans, who wanted to have a look at his 7ft 9in by 7ft 8in bedroom. 'The family have enjoyed living here for several years,' said a sympathetic neighbour, 'but they're fed up with it. This is the price Robbie has had to pay for his superstar status.'

Almost inevitably, matters came to a head the following year. Just as Jason had predicted, it was Robbie, not Gary, who was to be the catalyst for the break-up of the group, when he finally snapped in quite spectacular style. In mid-1995, supposedly clean-living Robbie turned up at Glastonbury with bleach-blond hair and a blacked-out tooth, waving champagne and cigarettes. Worse still, he was with Liam and Noel Gallagher, the volatile brothers behind Oasis. He was signing autographs, 'Robbie Williams, nutter'. Martin-Williams and the other four boys were appalled.

In retrospect, it is not difficult to see that this was almost bound to happen. Robbie was 21, had been buckling down since the age of 15, had been forced to put up an image as pure as the driven snow and was utterly fed up. A few tactful words somewhere would almost certainly have calmed the situation down and made everyone realise just what was at stake, not least because Robbie didn't want to leave Take That and Take That didn't want to split up. In the event, that was exactly what happened but no one seemed to realise that they had now danced right up to the edge.

This was actually the second time that Robbie had been to Glastonbury but the previous year, he'd spent the whole time hiding away in M People's tour bus. This time round, there wasn't a chance of missing him. 'I nicked sixteen bottles of champagne, put them in the boot of this blacked-out Jag and drove to Glastonbury,' he proclaimed. 'Drunk a bottle of champagne along the way.'

Robbie might not have meant to break away quite so spectacularly but, once he'd started, there was no stopping him. He was pictured with the boys from Pulp, played football with the Boo Radleys and cavorted with Simon from Menswear. Much of it was spent in a drunken haze but Robbie knew exactly what he was doing. 'Unauthorised TV interviews and photos were forbidden by our management,' he said. 'So at Glastonbury, I thought, "I'm going to do exactly what I want." I made sure I got my picture taken and I did every TV show in the place. I'd had enough.'

He certainly had: there was no way that his bandmates and manager could ignore what was happening now. And then, just to really ram the message home, he appeared on stage with Oasis. 'Liam just went, "Come on," and that was it, really,' he said. 'It's interesting though, isn't it? That's the moment when it [the conversion from pop to rock] actually crystallised.' As for Liam, although hostilities were soon to develop between the two, he was initially friendly. 'I walked in and Liam goes, "Take fucking what?" And that was it. I knew we'd have a laugh.'

It was, just as Jason had predicted, a delayed teenage rebellion, although rather more was at stake than in the usual adolescent meltdown. Robbie went on MTV's *Most Wanted* show and dropped his trousers for a bet. 'That's the most satisfying £10 I have ever earned,' he said. He turned up to an awards ceremony with his hair cut into Johnny Rotten-style blond spikes. He gave interviews that were essentially shoving two fingers up at the rest of them. 'I'm twenty-one. I'm in Britain's biggest band, but I'm bored out of my brains,' he said.

This was turning into a PR disaster, as Robbie prattled on about how fed up he was, how he'd had to turn down acting roles because of the band and how, given that they were kept under Nigel's thumb, it was very like being in the army. The boys were horrified and handled it about as badly as anyone could do. 'I came back and I was like, "Hi guys! Glastonbury was over the top! You're not gonna believe it! I was with Jarvis of Pulp, I was with Oasis, they're top!"' he said. 'I was like – and some fell on stony ground. They were like, "Really? Oh. Let's rehearse." So they had a meeting about my behaviour. Again.'

It was the end. Robbie disappeared again, leaving his bandmates utterly bewildered about what was going on. 'We don't know where Robbie is,' said Gary. 'We just want him to get in touch with us so we can tell him everything's OK.'

But it wasn't. In an interview on Radio 1 in July 1995, Mark let slip that, 'We had an agreement as a band to give six months' notice if anyone wanted to leave or fancied something different. He broke the news to us about two weeks ago. He gave us his six months' notice really. Since then, we have been trying to carry on in rehearsal but it was obvious he wasn't happy. So we decided maybe as a mate we didn't want to put him through this pain for six months and maybe he should go now.'

It was a very tactful way of glossing over the fact that Robbie had been sacked. Take That had originally been created as a four-piece, after all, so why not go back to Plan A? But no one seemed to have taken on board the fact that Robbie was one of the most popular members of Take That, and that this might – and did – cause the band's implosion. It was a mess.

Not that Robbie had planned this or even thought it through. Indeed, his initial reaction on being chucked out was terror: what was he going to do next? 'I was looking at all these faces and it was just like a whirl of, "What the fuck do I do in this situation?" This was never in my game plan,' Robbie said. 'And macho bravado came across to cover up. I was like, "Oh, you want me to go then? Well, can I take that melon?" Clutching the melon, Robbie went outside and climbed into the car with his driver, who took him back to Stoke-on-Trent. 'It was the weirdest journey that I've ever been on,' said Robbie, 'with these two people not knowing what to say or do and me not knowing whether to laugh, cry, throw myself out of the window – or phone up a few bands to see if they needed a vocalist. And that was it. The end of an era for me. And you know what? I don't even like melon.'

The rest of the band were pretty shocked, too. Mark was in tears. The fans were beside themselves:

one little girl tried (mercifully unsuccessfully) to kill herself. A hotline was set up that received hundreds of calls. It made the *News At Ten*; staff at *Boyz*, a light-hearted gay magazine, wore black armbands for a week.

The remaining boys tried to put a brave face on it. 'When Robbie first announced he wanted to leave, of course we were all devastated,' said Mark, who clearly was. 'We did even think about splitting up. But we love what we do so much and have so much to look forward to, with the new single and tour, that we feel we couldn't possibly call it a day.'

Gary also chipped in. 'The four of us are still a hundred per cent committed to this band and are very much looking forward to a long future together,' he said. The fans weren't so sure, shouting out Robbie's name when they appeared on *Top of the Pops*.

Robbie himself went to ground, heading to Carmarthen Bay holiday camp in Kidwelly, near Swansea, which was owned by Andrew Brown, a friend of his father. But it wasn't long before he began to come round. Though still in a state of shock and unsure about his future, he began to relish the fact that he could move around again without a minder, and that people were treating him normally once more. 'When I went home after being on the road with Take That, I would be totally lost,' he said. 'My mum would say, "Rob, what do you want for dinner?" and I'd be bemused. I never had to make decisions like that. On the road, I had people fannying around me the whole time.' And people did rally round: George Michael was one who gave him some advice.

But the question remained: what to do now? He was as popular as he ever had been, but no obvious career path lay in wait. In truth, the next few months were a blur: he hung out in London with Oasis, partied in St Tropez with George Michael, Bono, Paula Yates and Michael Hutchence. He was at every celebrity event going, drinking heavily and looking for a future. Robbie was free, but at a price.

And for all the bravado, he was feeling pretty bitter about the split from Take That. He bumped into his old bandmates at the Brit Awards in February 1996; it was not a success. Mark waved and said, 'Look after yourself.' The others ignored him. In actual fact, this also marked the break-up of Take That. There had been one last single, 'How Deep Is Your Love', but it wasn't working without Robbie. Anyway, Gary wanted a solo career. The

last concert was in Holland in April: with seven No
1s, four million singles and three million albums
behind them, Take That had split for ever. Or so
everyone thought.

Robbie made a few pointed remarks but his own
problems, specifically his drinking, were getting out
of control. 'I got drunk and fell over a lot. I wasn't
happy,' he said later that year. 'And I never had a
drink problem, no matter what the papers said. Not
having anything to do was the hardest thing. I let
myself waste away doing nothing and, for a while, I
bought into that rock 'n' roll thing. I jumped from
one myth to another. It was a security blanket.'

It was a very difficult time. Robbie wanted to
work but couldn't because of an impending law suit.
He would lash out one minute, calling Gary a
'clueless wanker' and the rest of them 'selfish,
arrogant and thick', then publicly apologise for
being unpleasant to them. It was mystifying to watch
from outside.

'I'm just very disappointed in the way he's turned
out,' Gary said. 'A lot of the things he's said in
articles have hurt us all – [that] he was a prisoner in
Take That, that none of us are close friends, that
we've never been friends. It's complete rubbish.
We're all so close and we always have been. He'd

always been Mark's best friend. Jason and Howard were a bit of a clan and Mark and Robbie were another. I would never join Mark and Robbie, I'd always join Jason and Howard because they were a little bit older. Mark grew up and became a very truthful, good-living person, I thought. And I think he left Robbie behind and Robbie resented that. We were doing dance routines on stage and Robbie was doing his own routine. We were afraid to say, "Robbie, you dickhead – fucking get it together. We're a five-piece band here." We couldn't do that any more – he was a bit of a loose cannon. He'd missed out on his teenage years and he wanted to live them now.'

Gary admitted that the boys were feeling a tad envious: they wanted to go out, get drunk and pull girls, too. But unlike Robbie, they toed the line. Rivalry now broke out. Robbie was finally able to release a single, a cover of George Michael's 'Freedom', on his new record label Chrysalis, with whom he'd signed a £2 million deal, while Gary released 'Forever Love'. Gary got to UK No 1, Robbie to No 2. The gloves were off.

Robbie was presenting a confident image but, behind the scenes, it was a different matter altogether. He had not, after all, chosen a solo career:

events had forced it upon him and it was a nerve-racking time. His first manager after Take That was Kevin Kinsella, who ran Jelly Street Management, and Robbie had stayed at his house in Cheshire after leaving the band. 'There were problems from the moment I took him on,' Kevin recalled. 'We met him off the plane, me and his mum, when he came back from George Michael's house in the South of France where he went after he'd been sacked. I got him home to my house and he just broke down crying. He was in a terrible state. He was living with us for three months, while the whole country's press was trying to find him. He was on drugs and booze and all messed up. At the time, he was probably on a bottle of vodka and a bottle of Bacardi a day. He was picking up these bottles and saying, "Can you get me more?"'

The association didn't last long – Robbie stayed with Kevin for just six months, during which time he did a stint on *The Big Breakfast*. A war of words with Gary began – 'I do wonder if the source of his feelings is financial, because I made much more than the rest of Take That,' said Gary smoothly, and it was true. At that stage, Gary had made about £6.5 million, as he got royalties for writing the band's songs, while the others had banked about £2.5

million each. Robbie gained a lot of weight; Gary did the opposite. There was increasing bitterness all round.

Robbie was becoming aware, though, that he was going to have to pull himself together. One person who helped him to do that was the Hon Jacqueline Hamilton-Smith. From an aristocratic background, Jacqui was not the most obvious partner for Robbie but she was, in fact, his first serious girlfriend. The pair met at a party given by her ex-boyfriend, record producer Nellee Hooper, late in 1995. At 29, she was 7 years older than Robbie and her mother Sonia, Lady Colwyn, was not too happy about their liaison. Asked if they would marry, she replied, 'He's only twenty-two and I really don't think he would be suitable. No, no, absolutely not.' Jacqui's father, Lord Colwyn, wasn't too pleased either, while Robbie's own family were a little disconcerted to find an aristocrat in their midst.

It was quite a serious relationship for a while (a few years after it ended, Jacqui married the actor Sean Pertwee) and she certainly provided him with some much-needed moral support while problems with the record label were sorted out. But by his own admission, Robbie's drinking and drug-taking were now totally out of control. Jacqui finished the relationship and, after a failed attempt by Robbie to woo her back, said she'd help him sort himself out – but only as a friend.

Other people were beginning to notice the state Robbie was in. One of these was Sir Elton John, who had been through something similar. On Elton's recommendation, Robbie went to see the celebrity therapist Beechy Colclough. He also found a new manager, Tim Abbot, who negotiated his release from RCA and his new deal with Chrysalis, but again the association did not last long. Robbie sacked him and, like Nigel Martin-Smith and Kevin Kinsella, he sued. (The case was eventually settled out of court.)

As it happened, his mother Jan had just retrained as a drugs counsellor, which at least gave her an insight into his problems. 'Take That gave Robbie a lot of experience, but it also took away his innocence,' she said in an interview at the time. 'He went in as a child and came out as a man. In the group, they were not allowed any opinions. Robbie was told to keep his mouth shut in interviews and not to take the spotlight away from Gary Barlow. He was in denial for such a long time. You can't treat somebody for drink and drug problems until they've addressed the issues themselves. It was only a few weeks ago when he admitted to himself what the rest of us knew, that he was able to get help. I couldn't counsel Robbie as a parent so that's when Elton put him in touch with Beechy Colclough.'

But matters continued to worsen. Robbie was binge drinking and binge eating: his weight had shot up to 13 stone from a previous 11. He was now being sued by three managers and he was in danger of entering a downward spiral from which he would not emerge. Friends were increasingly concerned, not least when Robbie embarked on a three-day bender. 'He [Robbie] started on Friday night and finished on Sunday morning, slumped on a friend's floor,' said an onlooker. 'Robbie drank solidly throughout. He can really stick it away and, once he's on a roll, there's no stopping him. Elton says they are very similar characters. He would binge drink for days and then collapse in a heap – just like Robbie.'

In the end, Elton's advice prevailed and Robbie returned to Colclough. He took the situation seriously and began to face up to his problems. He started to lose weight, and also got back in touch with Mark. But as 1997 dawned, Robbie was still not clear exactly where he was going. Work had begun on his first solo album, *Life Thru a Lens* (originally titled *The Show Off Must Go On*), but there was no indication he was about to become a major star. Robbie still had some way to go before he was out of the woods.

CHAPTER FOUR

A SOLO STAR
IS BORN

L ittle did he know it but Robbie Williams was
about to turn into one of the country's biggest
stars in years. Still only 22, he was pulling himself
together, putting the bingeing behind him and getting
on with his life. His former bandmates were about to
plunge into years of obscurity, little suspecting that
one day they would become one of the most popular
bands in Britain again, and that they would be
reunited with their old friend. But at that stage, early
1997, the shadows of the first incarnation of Take
That were still hanging heavy over the erstwhile
band members. In April, Gary and Robbie were
again pitched head to head.

It made for great publicity, of course, but the effects
it must have had on the two young men can only be

guessed at. First, Robbie released 'Old Before I Die'; two weeks later, Gary put out a single written by Madonna, 'Love Won't Wait'. Exactly the same thing happened: Gary got to UK No 1 and Robbie achieved UK No 2. Robbie kept his head down, kept working on the new album and grew a beard (mercifully short lived). There was, however, a return to drinking and drug-taking, which necessitated another spell in rehab, although Robbie was nearing the stage when he was finally going to give it all up for good. Chrysalis, which had a lot riding on Robbie, issued a statement, saying it was, 'entirely supportive of any decision Robbie may have taken in regard to his own wellbeing. We believe Robbie is, without a doubt, a great talent and he has the depth and diversity to become the brightest star of his generation. We are delighted with the as yet unmixed songs which have been filtering out of the studio and predict the album contains many singles, which will drive the campaign through into 1998.'

They were to be proved right, but not immediately. Robbie's third single, 'Lazy Days', was released in July and only made it to UK No 8. Robbie was looking a little better, though. Newly out of rehab, he was off the booze and drugs, taking some exercise and beginning to mull over plans to tour when *Life Thru a Lens* was released in September. There was no special woman (though a lot of unspecial ones) but Robbie was now flirting with a slightly more dangerous take on his sexuality. 'I could sleep with a bloke today,' he told one interviewer. 'But I actually don't want to. I might do it tomorrow. I've no qualms.' And so on in that vein, which led, absolutely inevitably, to speculation that Robbie was gay. Take That's time in gay nightclubs continued to fuel the rumours, too. In fact, Robbie was totally straight but couldn't resist edging the speculation along.

When the album was released, both it and the accompanying tour garnered good reviews and sales, although there was the odd stunt that backfired. Robbie went through a lengthy period of stripping off in public and, in October, upset some fans by leaving the stage at the Manchester Academy, taking his clothes off, singing a final song in the nude and then mooning rather than bowing. Not everyone was impressed. The war of words with Gary continued, although strangely they did appear on stage together in December 1997, at Princess Diana's Concert of Hope. Appearing in front of 6,000 fans at Battersea Power Station in south London, the two embraced on stage. But the truce was not to last.

That concert, however, heralded the move that

was to take Robbie from popular performer to superstar. He sang six numbers, including his latest single, which he dedicated to the late Princess. That song was called 'Angels' and was for ever more to be associated with Princess Diana. It was also to make Robbie a massive star.

'Angels' came about through collaborating with 33-year-old songwriter Guy Chambers, who had come to the attention of IE Management. IE was looking after Robbie and trying to find a songwriting partner for their young charge: from the moment the two young men met, they hit it off. For the next few years, Guy would write the music and Robbie the lyrics; the first of these was 'Angels'. Strangely, considering it is probably Robbie's most famous single, it only ever reached UK No 4, although it spent 13 weeks in the charts in total. Robbie also won over a new generation of fans when he sung it live on *Top of the Pops* and an appearance on Parkinson followed.

'Angels' did something else, too. It turned the album from which it was taken, *Life Thru a Lens*, from a respectable seller into a massive hit, and eventually, UK No 1. Robbie, by now having a brief fling with Spice Girl Melanie Chisholm, was thrilled but, unfortunately, celebrated by falling off the wagon once more. He went on a very public marathon bender at London's Groucho Club, necessitating subsequent apologies and the acceptance of something else: Robbie was never going to be the kind of person who could enjoy the occasional drink. It was all or nothing and he was ultimately going to have to give up for good.

Gary's debut album, *Open Road*, was also to get to UK No 1 but the different levels of success the former bandmates were to experience was now beginning to emerge. Robbie was beginning to make headlines with everything he did, from stripping off to revealing that one track, 'Hello, Sir', was written to get back at a teacher at school who had reduced him to tears. (The teacher in question, Steve Cartlidge, sounded pretty amused by it all.)

The fling with Mel C was a brief one but Robbie was now about to embark on the second serious relationship in his life. He sang at the Noel Coward tribute concert to raise money to fight AIDS and also on the bill was the girl band All Saints. One of its members, Nicole Appleton, caught his eye. The two had met once before but this time it clicked and it wasn't long before they were openly admitting to be a couple. It became so serious that the two of them even discussed having a child.

Indeed, as 'Let Me Entertain You', his sixth solo single, got to UK No 3, Robbie was bubbling over with happiness. 'She's the one,' he said of Nicole. 'We're getting on very well together and we're happy.' Indeed, so happy were they that, in June 1998, they got engaged, with Robbie going down on bended knee just before a solo concert at the Royal Albert Hall.

It was not to be. Much later, Nicole revealed that there had been some heartbreak even in the happy early days: she'd discovered that she was pregnant, and a delighted Robbie was only too happy that he was going to be a dad. He wrote a song about his unborn baby, which appears on the *I've Been Expecting You* album. All Saints, however, were still going strong and the record company was not amused. Nicole ended up having a termination. That scarred the relationship permanently and eventually the engagement was called off. Robbie was devastated and fell off the wagon again (which, in truth, he had been doing anyway).

At least his career was soaring. In 1998, Prince Charles asked Robbie what he would have had to cancel to attend the Prince's bash at the Lyceum. Nothing, said Robbie, apart from world domination. A key part of his appeal was his vulnerability. The much publicised drink and drugs episodes, the genuine distress when his relationships broke down – all these spoke of a man who might have the world at his feet but sometimes needed a hug. There was a 'little boy lost' quality to Robbie that made him immensely appealing in many people's eyes. On Christmas Day 1998, his father Pete joined him on stage: they sang a duet, the Frank Sinatra song 'That's Life'. For a while after that, Pete also had his share of screaming girls.

Robbie was able to mock himself, too. At the beginning of 1999, he was off on tour again: a montage at the beginning of the show included newspaper headlines such as, HOW DRINK AND DRUGS... and WHO ATE ALL THE PIES? He would confide in his audience about his hurt over Nicole. He would flirt with his audience and tease them. Here was a man who was born to be on stage.

In February 1999, Robbie was nominated for a record-breaking six Brit Awards, winning three of them and consolidating his position as the country's most popular entertainer. That sense of humour certainly hadn't gone: a fellow winner was Fatboy Slim, who held up a card saying, 'Speechless'. Robbie held up one saying, 'Legless'. The audience loved it. For the first time, tattoos began to appear on his body and he took a break in the US, which, significantly, he enjoyed because everyone left him alone.

He still wasn't entirely off the booze, however, and there were flashes of arrogance, as when he went to collect the Best Male Artist award at the MTV awards. Robbie snatched the trophy out of George Michael's hands, saying, 'Damn right!' But the roguishness was still there: it emerged that he'd appeared, heavily disguised, as an extra in *EastEnders* and *Only Fools and Horses*, the latter providing a clue as to his identity because he was leaning against a jukebox playing 'Could It Be Magic' by Take That.

In the background, throughout all this, the litigation had been continuing. In the end, Robbie lost his battle with Nigel Martin-Smith, to whom he was ordered to pay £1 million. Robbie was livid but at least the case was over. Even so, Robbie called off the rest of the dates of his tour. This raised eyebrows in some quarters, not least from Sir Elton John, but what could anyone do? Robbie was an adult now: it was up to him how he behaved.

As he had done so often in the past, Robbie pushed himself to the brink and then stepped back again. Just when the industry started to fear he'd implode, he went back to work. He was still raw about his split from Nicole (and had started a vicious war of words with the Gallagher brothers, especially Liam, although he and Nicole were not yet an item) but Robbie was never one to stay away from women for long. He was now actively pursuing Andrea Corr and making some headway: the two were spotted getting very cosy over lunch. It wasn't long, however, before that came to nothing: Andrea finally turned him down. There was further hurt in store when Nicole criticised him publicly, saying, 'I would never have children with him.' Only Robbie and a few select others would have understood why that cut would have been deep.

The United States, too, continued to resist his charms. Robbie has made several attempts to crack it over the years, never successfully, and he was having one now: *The Ego Has Landed* (not a good idea for an album title in America) never got higher than No 85 in the *Billboard* charts, and 'Millennium' didn't even make the Top 100. But back home and in Europe and Asia, he was comprehensively adored.

With the constant attention, the adulation and the rest of it, Robbie's world had become a madhouse. Even a much more stable and sober person would have found it difficult to cope. The feud with Gary rumbled on. 'They fired me … and I went on to sell six million records and tour America,' he cried out to one audience. 'So fuck them! I'm the greatest release Take That ever had!'

It was beginning to get to Gary. His own solo career was not going according to plan, but Robbie, who was never meant to amount to anything very much, was doing spectacularly well. The fact that Robbie was now gloating so openly just served to make it worse. 'It's annoying for me that he's the one who has gone forward and done it,' Gary admitted. 'I can't believe it. I can only think he must have a good team around him – like he had in the past. I was with him for seven years and never saw him write a song. It was hard enough for me to get him to sing. I don't talk to Robbie, never have. I don't understand it. He's engineered the whole situation. This so-called row between us is all unprovoked by me. I'm still trying to understand it.'

Robbie's popularity – and bank balance – continued to soar. By 1999, he was estimated to be worth about £10 million, significantly more than he had left Take That with (and significantly more than the other members of Take That) but still he could not help but lash out at the others. 'The band had the creativity of mentally unstable morons and was spawned by Satan,' was one typical outburst. 'The manager Nigel Martin-Smith really mucked me up emotionally. He managed me and manipulated me from when I was sixteen. It was a Devil's pact – he gave you fame and riches, you gave him your soul and twenty-five per cent of the takings. OK, I got the riches and fame but I had no respect for what I did. I hated our lead singer Gary Barlow and I hated our music. In the end, I hated myself.'

This was not only unfair but a wild exaggeration of what had gone on in the past, but Robbie had been hurt by the treatment meted out to him. Both personally and professionally, his feelings had been dented and, for a person who was far more insecure than he usually admitted, it had been a damaging time.

But in other ways, life was good. He'd moved into a £3.4 million mansion in London's Notting Hill, which he shared with his childhood friend Jonathan Wilkes. He sang at the wedding of Guy Chambers and signed a £2 million deal to promote Pepsi. Success in the United States continued to elude him, however, and perhaps it was no wonder. As 3,000 fans were taking their seats at a concert in Atlanta, Robbie wandered out on stage stark naked, his hands alone covering his modesty, before pretending he'd taken a wrong turn and heading back to his dressing room. Britain still loved him, though – 'She's the One' went straight to UK No 1.

Still the feuding continued: when not with Gary, with Oasis. After that earlier honeymoon period, relations had soured between them massively, with Noel calling him a 'fat dancer'. Robbie responded by sending him a funeral wreath bearing the legend, 'To Noel Gallagher, RIP. Heard your latest album – with deepest sympathy, Robbie Williams.' Liam did not take it well: 'You can tell the cunt, if I ever see him in a club in London, I'm gonna break his fucking nose. He'll be needing wreaths on the door! Rest in peace!'

Robbie appeared at the Brits, where he won Best Video and Best Single. 'Would anyone like to see me fight Liam?' he inquired as he accepted the award. 'Would you pay to come and see it? Liam, a hundred grand of your money and a hundred grand of my money. We can have a fight and we can all watch it on TV. Now what are you going to do?' Back down was the answer, with Liam muttering, 'Childish,' and, 'Not what rock 'n' roll is about.'

These Brits put Robbie in the record books: having won a total of nine, he had now overtaken Annie Lennox's eight. He was also still single, a brief romance with the TV presenter Tania Strecker having come to nothing. He admitted to having the hots for Kylie Minogue and, in 2000, the two recorded the duet 'Kids' together – although on a personal level, Kylie turned him down.

Robbie did some work for UNICEF, bought and sold a silver Ferrari (he didn't have a driving licence) and courted controversy with the video for his latest single 'Rock DJ', another UK No 1. He actually made two videos for it, one innocuous and even a little tedious, and the other repulsive. In it, he plays a DJ spinning discs and being totally ignored by the beautiful women around him; to get their attention he starts stripping off (natch) and, as they continue to ignore him, he starts clawing off his own flesh and throwing it at them. They finally turn on him and gorge on the flesh until all that is left is a dancing skeleton. It made quite a difference from the video for 'She's the One', which showed him ice skating. There was no way it could be shown on prime-time television, but it achieved its purpose, namely massive publicity.

Booze, however, was still leading to extremely erratic behaviour. There was one episode when Robbie and actor Nick Moran went to Stringfellows: Robbie stripped off, joined the dancers on stage and, after the bouncers told him to sit down, had a panic attack and disappeared. Moran, left with the £300 bill, was livid, although Robbie did later send him a bottle of champagne and £300 – in Monopoly money.

In the wake of that, Robbie managed to stay sober for a couple of weeks, only to learn that his ex, Nicole, had hooked up with Liam Gallagher – something Robbie saw as a total betrayal. He went to the South of France to lick his wounds, with none other than Geri Halliwell, then in the middle of her transformation from voluptuous Ginger Spice to stick-thin solo performer.

If Robbie wanted to get the world's attention, he certainly succeeded. There was a huge amount of speculation as to whether he and Geri were a couple, while the two were clearly revelling in it all. Geri gave almost daily displays of yoga on the beach, while Robbie sat around showing off his tattoos. The two of them jet skied around the Mediterranean, before having a public row in a restaurant one night and a public display of togetherness the next day. The other Spice girls warned Geri about Robbie – they'd witnessed his treatment of Mel C at first hand – while those in the know murmured that the reality was that he was not over Nicole.

But professionally he continued to soar. He had a new album, *Sing When You're Winning*, out that autumn, and posed naked with the Brazilian model Gisele for the September issue of *Vogue*. 'Kids' (which caused controversy with a reference to sodomy that was cut in the version that appeared on Kylie's album) got to UK No 2. He won an MTV award for 'Rock DJ'. But then the news broke that Nicole was pregnant by Liam and the strain, yet again, began to tell: Robbie stormed out of the Q Awards in October close to tears when Liam called him 'queer'. More seriously still, after a raucous performance at the MTV Awards, in which he was seen dancing on the tables, yelling, 'Party, party, I am the king! Now let's rock this place!' He then got into a set-to with record producer Nellee Hooper and then collapsed, foaming at the mouth.

Something was clearly very wrong. A fellow guest, Andreas Lundberg, had witnessed it all: 'The party was well under way when Robbie jumped on the table with Wyclef Jean,' he said. 'He was wild-eyed but seemed to be enjoying himself as they sang two songs together. He moved towards the crowd, who were all around him, cheering. One of them handed him a glass of beer. He took it and had a drink. Then he swayed a bit and all of a sudden Robbie fell down.

No one had any idea what was happening. One minute he seemed lively and the next he collapsed. I caught a quick look at his face and he did not look very well. But no one could get near him. The bodyguards kept everyone away and rushed him out the back.'

Another person in the crowd was Jonathan Wilkes, who was heard earlier telling his friend, 'Come on, Rob – you've had enough now.'

That was the last occasion on which Robbie had a drink. He flew to Barbados, calmed down and turned over a new leaf. But he had certainly not lost the talent to shock. Once back in Britain, he gave an interview about his holiday with Geri, saying they didn't sleep together and, 'I'm gay anyway,' and then outed himself when he was in Paris. 'I am now officially known as Roberta Williams,' he said. He was joking but his record company told him to pipe down, as not everyone got his sense of humour. Robbie complied and, in 2001, had his most successful year to date.

It started with relocating to LA. Robbie's failure to crack the United States was turning into a blessing in disguise. The fact that he could walk around unrecognised meant that it was the ideal place to escape the stresses and strains that were ever-present

Top left: Slim before he was winning, a young Robbie Williams shows that unmistakable grin.

Top right: Gary Barlow and admirers.   © *PA Photos*

Bottom: Take That in 1992 – Gary Barlow, Howard Donald, Jason Orange, Mark Owen and Robbie Williams.   © *Rex Features*

Top: At the Hammersmith Apollo, London, in 1992.   © *Rex Features*

Bottom: Early Take That photocalls. The group caused an international storm, though later Robbie compared being in the band to working in your favourite shop but having to 'clean up the dog turd outside'.

Stage gear designed to
get maximum attention.
© *PA Photos*

Top: Take That in America.

© *PA Photos*

Bottom: A 1991 shot of the band at the Majestic Ballroom in Reading.

© *Rex Features*

Top: The band with manager Nigel Martin-Smith. © *PA Photos*

Bottom: Take That with Beatles producer George Martin. © *Rex Features*

Top: Robbie hangs out with Liam Gallagher at Glastonbury.
An appearance that worsened relations with Take That.

Bottom: A Robbie-less Take That at the 1996 Brit Awards.
Max Beesley plays percussion.

© *Rex Features*

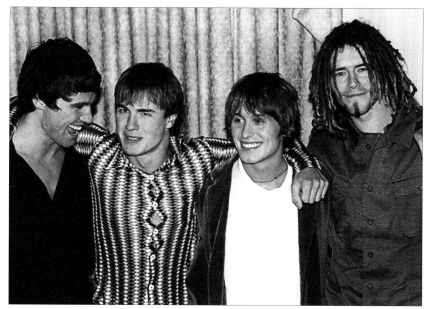

Top: Nobody really knows how spicy Robbie's relationship with former Spice Girl Geri Halliwell was, but their holidays and public appearances together caused huge speculation.

Bottom: Take That announcing their breakup in Manchester.   © *Rex Features*

Top: Prince Charming. Robbie meets Prince Charles with Geri to celebrate The Prince of Wales's 50th Birthday.

© *Alpha Press*

Bottom: A right royal mess. Robbie enjoys a food fight with Patsy Kensit on her birthday.

© *Rex Features*

in the UK. He joined the LA branch of Alcoholics Anonymous and started settling down, something that was helped by the fact that Geri was out there as well. But the strains of life were still there: he was attacked while on stage in Stuttgart. A mentally ill fan, aged 20, jumped on stage and punched Robbie, hurling him into the pit that separated the stage from the audience before security men got him under control.

Robbie was extremely shocked but coped magnificently. He clambered back on the stage and announced, 'We can't let an idiot like that spoil our joy tonight. I'm carrying on for you.' This was greeted with a massive round of applause, as well it should have been, although Robbie did increase his security after that.

Another slew of awards followed at that year's Brits, at which Robbie requested an alcohol-free table and was presented with Best British Male Solo Artist by Geri ('According to the press, he has been giving me one, so now I'm going to give him one,' she quipped), bringing his tally up to 12. There was still no constant woman in his life, though, with (totally false) rumours now surfacing about his relationship with Jonathan Wilkes. The reality was that they were childhood friends and that Jonathan was one of the few people Robbie could really trust, but they couldn't resist encouraging some of the speculation themselves.

Robbie also encouraged speculation about his relationship with Geri, twice saying that they were friends who sleep together and then twice denying it. Then he said he wore his tiger-decorated Y-fronts in bed with her. Whatever the truth, it was to mark the end of their friendship. Geri appeared to be getting increasingly fed up. 'I am out with Robbie Williams a lot but he is *not* my boyfriend and we are *not* a couple,' she said. The two then ignored one another at the Capital FM awards – despite sitting at the same table. There were rumours that Geri was jealous of a fling Robbie had had with Rod Stewart's daughter Kimberly.

Robbie tried to placate her. In an appearance on the *Parkinson* show, he said he loved Geri. He sent her presents of clothing and jewellery to try to make up. But he'd gone too far, telling Radio 1, 'Geri and I are just good friends who have the occasional shag.' Geri was livid. 'I can't stand men in tight, tiny underpants with animal designs on them,' she said. 'I prefer blokes in a cute pair of boxer shorts. I find that much more attractive. Robbie is a real turn-off in those things but he would try anything for a laugh.'

It was evidently a tough moment for Robbie. After

his next single – a cover of Queen's 'We Are the Champions' – came 'Eternity', about a summer spent holidaying with a beautiful woman. 'It's for the little yoga girl,' he said.

Another album followed, *Swing When You're Winning*, featuring some classic songs by the likes of Frank Sinatra, along with a duet with Nicole Kidman, 'Something Stupid' (his fifth UK No 1). But for the first time, he appeared to wish to heal the rift with his ex-bandmates. 'I saw one of those programmes the other night – *I Love 1993* – and there was a big piece on it about Take That,' he said. 'It really upset me – really, really upset me. Howard and Mark were speaking and they just looked really sad about the whole thing. You could see it in their eyes. I just went to my back garden and had a cry.' The beginnings of the thoughts of reconciliation had taken place – and this was 2001.

Robbie played at the Royal Albert Hall, duetting with Jonathan Wilkes at one stage, singing 'Me and My Shadow' and joking about being gay. (The record company was forced to clarify that he was actually straight and that Wilkes had a girlfriend.) But although he had been spending time in the UK, Europe and Asia, his heart these days really did lie in America.

By 2002, Robbie was spending an increasing amount of time in the US. It was at around this time that Robbie became involved in *Nobody, Someday*, a documentary about his life, filmed largely when he was on tour. The person who actually made the documentary, Brian Hill, recalled their first meeting. 'What struck me was that he was never on his own,' he said. 'I got to his flat and there were all these other people around him – security, PA and various other people. He saw me as another person who wanted a piece of him.

'He didn't know who I was or what I wanted. He turned to his PA in front of me and said, "Why are we having a meeting about a documentary? There are always cameras following me around." He hadn't even spoken to me at this point and he was saying all this right in my earshot. But when we spoke, I think he liked the fact that I was interested in the downside of what he does. He saw it as an opportunity to unburden himself.'

In the end, the two men got along famously, producing a documentary that really did show the downside of being the world's most famous pop star. Brian was also able to witness at first hand the fact that Robbie was winning his battle with drink and drugs. 'He didn't stop anyone from having a drink,' he said. 'But they were very strict about drug-taking. Anybody caught using drugs would be sent home. He admitted he didn't know whether he would make it without relapsing. It is really difficult to go around Europe and get up on stage every night and stay sober and not take drugs. But he did it. Robbie was very strong about it. I never once heard him say, "I could do with a drink," or, "I really want some drugs." He was pleased that he kept clean.'

It was a major achievement and Robbie determined that it would be a turning point in his life. And so it was that he finally decided to move to Los Angeles, to escape the kind of success that had taken such a comprehensive toll on his life. It was announced that he would take six months off and so, accompanied by the loyal Jonathan Wilkes, Robbie uprooted himself to LA, where he rented a £12,000-a-month ranch-style house in the Hollywood Hills from the actor Dan Aykroyd.

But not everything was going entirely smoothly. Legal arguments had surrounded the lyrics of 'Jesus in a Camper Van' and, in February, they were finally resolved: Robbie, Guy Chambers and EMI were ordered to pay more than £250,000 to settle royalties, costs and interest. The song the lyrics had been borrowed from turned out to be Woody

Guthrie's 1961 song called, 'I Am the Way', as well as a later offering from Loudon Wainwright III. The judge, however, was extremely sympathetic to Robbie, saying, 'I have been in very grave doubt as to who actually won these proceedings,' and added that the copyright infringement was not 'cynical or flagrant'.

But Robbie had other things on his mind, not least his love life. The first encounter between Robbie and Rachel Hunter, the estranged wife of Rod Stewart, came in a nightclub called Tangier, where the two exchanged phone numbers. 'That's why I love LA,' said Robbie happily. 'There's a hot blonde on every corner – I never want to leave.' It was not, however, to lead immediately to a relationship. They had simply met and liked one another. That, for now, was that.

Robbie was also showing that he had lost none of his self-deprecating sense of humour with the move. A video shown at the Brits, when Robbie won Best British Male, proved that. 'Hello, Will, from Pop Idol,' he announced from a perch by his swimming pool, as he waved his award in the air. 'You think you can take this away from me? Well, you can't. Three times I've won this, man, and you haven't got it. I'm much too strong for you. You want to take the food off my table. You want to stop my kids going to school. I don't think so. Craig [David] couldn't do it – what makes you think you can take it away from me?' And then, 'Good luck, mate. I think you're great.' Not that Robbie had any reason to feel insecure – he had now won 13 Brit awards, more than twice as many as any other male star since the awards began 21 years earlier.

Robbie did, however, make one trip back to the UK: to see Jonathan Wilkes's debut in *Godspell* in Edinburgh. The relationship between the two was as strong as ever. 'It's very special,' said Jonathan. 'We are like brothers. We've pulled each other out of loads of scrapes. He is one of the most talented writers in the business, which is very useful as he tells me when my songs are rubbish.' Jonathan was about to settle down: he had just become engaged to Nikki Wheeler, a dancer.

In the background, however, trouble was looming from a direction no one had foreseen – Guy Chambers. Robbie and Guy had been working so well as a partnership that it seemed to have occurred to no one, including the two men themselves, that a rift between them could ever emerge – but it did. And the train of events, once begun, quickly escalated out of control.

The first intimation of trouble ahead was when it was announced that Guy was going to be working with Will Young – the same Will Young who Robbie had warned off at the Brit awards. That had only been in jest, of course, but this new development was too close for comfort. While Robbie might have been prepared to welcome his younger rival on to the stage, he had no desire at all to lose pole position.

EMI wasn't too thrilled about this latest turn of events either, nor were they particularly happy about Robbie's new life generally, especially a new circle of friends that included Marilyn Manson and Ozzy Osbourne. It appeared that Robbie was becoming interested in a very different world, one that would not necessarily appeal to his fans.

That said, EMI was determined to hang on to its star entertainer. Other record companies had let it be known that they would top any bid when Robbie's next record contract came up for renewal, and the fact that EMI did not have quite the clout in the US that it had elsewhere, provided further impetus for Robbie to look around. He was clearly savouring the situation. 'We are doing the rounds of the record companies to see what each is offering,' said David Enthoven, Robbie's manager. 'The profile in America is certainly a consideration but we're looking for the best deal overall. There is nothing more I can say as we're in the middle of the negotiating process.' And that, for then, was that.

CHAPTER FIVE

ROBBIE GETS ROMANTIC

As the stakes rose in the background, another element of Robbie's life was beginning to come to the notice of the public. After an initial meeting with Rachel Hunter, it was becoming clear that the two got on very well indeed. In fact, they got on so well that it appeared they were now a couple. 'Rachel's the happiest she has been in years,' said a friend. 'She went through a very low patch earlier in the year, when she felt very depressed, isolated and lonely, but Robbie has changed that. The Rachel we're seeing now is brimming with confidence and is excited about her new relationship.'

As, indeed, they both were. It was not long before they were seen constantly in one another's company: bowling, watching baseball and going on dates.

Robbie met Rachel's children, Renee and Liam. And he was prepared to talk about it: 'She's gorgeous and a great comfort to me,' he said. 'We've been through a lot and talk about anything and everything. We've been seeing each other for a while and we're there for each other through thick and thin.' The *News of the World* then pictured the two of them canoodling, in a set of pictures in which they started clothed and ended in a state of undress. As it emerged that they knew they were being watched, it caused an outcry. But this relationship, like all the others, was not to last.

Matters were better with his career. Negotiations had been going on for months and finally came to a conclusion in October. With Rachel by his side, Robbie flew back to London to sign a record-breaking deal for a cool £80 million, twice the £40 million that had originally been on offer. It was a staggering amount and made headlines as such: £10 million up front, £15 million on completion of the first album – *Escapology*, which had been recorded over the summer – and £55 million for the next three. In return EMI got a percentage of Robbie's merchandising, publishing rights and live performances, which made it a very unusual contract. 'I'm rich beyond my wildest dreams,' said Robbie with commendable understatement.

But it wasn't all rejoicing for Robbie. The deal created huge expectations for him to live up to, on top of which he had still not broken the States. 'I'm not saying that Robbie has peaked, but he's certainly plateaued and it's a question of where you go from there,' said Tim Abbot, Robbie's first manager as a solo act. Indeed, with the timing that always seems to be a feature of any major announcement, a crisis made itself felt almost immediately. The simmering row with Guy Chambers finally came to the boil – and the two parted ways.

The timing couldn't have been worse. All eyes were on Robbie: he'd signed one of the biggest deals in the music industry's history and observers were just waiting for a problem to raise its ugly head. The reason for the split was simple: Robbie wanted total commitment from everyone who worked with him to the extent that they wouldn't work with anyone else (the fact that Guy had worked with Will Young had clearly touched a nerve). Guy, on the other hand, wanted to collaborate with other people, so he refused to sign a deal that meant he could only work with Robbie. A furious Robbie released an immediate press statement: 'Robbie Williams wishes Guy Chambers the best of luck with his band The Licks.' The band in question were complete unknowns: Robbie was clearly making a point.

There were hurt feelings on both sides. 'Guy has decided to work with other people and on other projects,' said a spokesman, playing down the rift. 'After six years and five albums, he feels it is time to move on. *Escapology* is finished and Guy has co-written twelve of the fourteen songs. He feels he is bowing out on a creative high.'

In November, *Escapology* was released and relieved everyone at EMI by going straight in at UK No 1. Shortly afterwards, the single 'Feel' followed, accompanied by a video featuring Daryl Hannah and, while it didn't quite top the charts, it achieved a commendable UK No 4. Matters were helped by *Escapology*'s position in the annual charts – despite its release in November 2003, it still ranked as the highest-selling album of the year.

By the end of 2003, Robbie had become a seriously wealthy man. At the beginning of the year, he had ranked 962 in the *Sunday Times* Rich List. By the end of the year, he had jumped to number 504 with an estimated £68 million in the bank – higher than George Michael. However, romantically, he remained as troubled as ever. In January 2003, reports had begun to emerge that his relationship with Rachel was on the rocks. These were originally denied, until fresh stories came out to the effect that Rachel had left Robbie on the eve of his 29th birthday. Whatever the truth, they were certainly an item no more, the split being blamed on Robbie's demanding personality.

Robbie continued to try to break the US but it didn't work. *Escapology* did not receive such rave reviews across the Atlantic as it had in Britain, with some critics claiming Robbie's very 'Englishness' worked against him. But the rest of the world continued to love him and Robbie took his inability to crack the US market on the chin, saying he didn't really care. 'I don't think the album will break here, no,' he announced. 'To tell you the truth, I don't want it badly enough, which sort of defeats the purpose. My ego says, "Go and do it." But the part of me that wants to become a father and raise kids and have some sort of normalcy says, "What the fuck are you doing? No one knows who you are here, and that's great." Then the ego comes back and says, "Try to make it happen." But to tell the truth, it's not going to happen for me here. I could break this place. If I toured here it would solve everything because the live show is great. But I'm not prepared to work that hard.'

As time went on, Robbie's life continued to change and progress. Perhaps the biggest change of all came about in February 2004, when Jonathan Wilkes finally tied the knot. Despite the years of rumour and speculation surrounding his relationship with Robbie, the truth was now clear: they were simply extremely good friends. But delighted as Robbie was for his long-term chum, it was inevitable that Jonathan's new matrimonial status would cause an upheaval in Robbie's life.

That year, Robbie turned 30, a significant milestone. He had been in LA on his birthday but, in March, he invited 50 friends and family to an official party, which was celebrated in Skibo Castle in Scotland, where Madonna and Guy Ritchie had got married. It was a restrained an affair. 'We were all on milkshakes,' one of the guests, Max Beesley, revealed, and much of the three-day stay was spent playing golf. Other guests included Ant and Dec. Robbie declared he was in love with the Highland scenery and wore a tweed jacket and deerstalker.

But shortly after that, Robbie's past began to resurrect itself, demonstrating in the process quite how far he'd come. It had been nine years since Robbie had left Take That and the band had disintegrated shortly afterwards – remembered, it seemed, only for launching the solo career of one R Williams. Now, however, it began to emerge that there was still real interest in the band and, to the astonishment of all concerned, a real chance that they would reform, albeit only briefly, at the end of the year. Interviews and a television special were planned, and the group and its members were welcomed back into the public eye as warmly as if they'd never been away.

There was intense interest in what the individual band members had been up to in the intervening years, but all that was overshadowed by one question: would Robbie be part of the reunion? In the years since leaving the band, there had been no end of barbed remarks about his former colleagues and their former manager Nigel Martin-Smith.

It soon became clear that Robbie would participate in some way, although it was the Robbie of the past, not Robbie today, who would be on show. Old material was coming out again and, of course, it featured Robbie in the days before he left Take That. 'The band's record label BMG came to us with the idea of releasing live footage of their old concerts,' said Martin-Smith, who was contracted as co-producer. 'It was obvious that there's still a lot of interest in the band – and none of the footage has ever been put out. So we agreed to put out a live DVD – complete with Robbie.'

But would Robbie take part in the reunion? 'There's more chance of Hell freezing over,' said the man himself. It was clear the bitterness still ran very deep. Over time, Robbie had come to forgive hurtful behaviour on the part of his fellow band members, and, later in the year, when the rest of the band reunited for a television special, he sent a video message apologising for his own hurtful comments and wishing them the best. He also had started to pay tribute to them at his concerts and had shared the stage with Mark for a rendition of 'Back for Good'.

And he was also adding other strings to his bow. A film called *De-Lovely* was about to be released, a biopic of the great American songwriter Cole Porter starring Kevin Kline and Ashley Judd. Robbie had a cameo role in it as a wedding singer and performed the song 'It's De-Lovely', which so impressed the film's director Irwin Winkler that he forecast Robbie could have a future as a film star.

'He was so successful in this movie that, when we do the TV slots to promote the film, we're using scenes of him singing "De-Lovely",' Winkler said. 'He's really great. I picked him for the film because I had seen a TV special and knew he could do it. Then I saw this photo of him with tattoos all over his body and he was kind of grungy-looking, but when I met him I was surprised because he's a gentle guy. He came along to the studios and put on a tuxedo – which hid all his tattoos – and he looked great. I really want to use him again. I'd love to and I'm thinking of doing another musical. It would be such a joy.'

But, of course, there was still business to be taken care of. The run-up had begun to the release of his *Greatest Hits*, which was due to feature songs from *Life Thru a Lens*, *I've Been Expecting You*, *Sing When You're Winning* and *Escapology*, as well as two new tracks entitled 'Radio' and 'Miss Understood'. The latter song was also due to feature in the second Bridget Jones film, *The Edge of Reason*. (Robbie had contributed two songs – 'Have You Met Miss Jones?' and 'Not of This Earth' – to the first movie.)

In autumn that year came the publication of *Feel*, an authorised glimpse into the court of King Robbie, by the journalist Chris Heath. The pages rippled with the sound of scores being settled: Noel Gallagher, Nigel Martin-Smith and Gary Barlow were just some of the people to get blasted. Among a good deal else, Robbie also revealed that Gary used to charge his fellow Take That members £1 to use his mobile phone.

Robbie also confessed that the shots of him and Rachel Hunter had, indeed, been staged, and took the opportunity to have yet another go at Noel Gallagher, who had once so famously labelled him as 'the fat dancer from Take That'. Revenge was clearly exceedingly sweet – Oasis had broken various musical records by holding two gigs at Knebworth until Robbie trumped them with the triple.

Finally, for good measure, Robbie announced that he had never been in love. Indeed, the only real love he'd ever felt, he said, was towards one Rachel Gilson, who he'd known from the old days in Stoke-on-Trent. She was the first, Robbie explained, and he still had feelings for her. Unfortunately, she had another boyfriend.

There were also signs that Robbie was beginning to get tired of some of the elements of his past, and that became increasingly clear when a newspaper published a story alleging that he'd had gay trysts when he was a member of Take That. In the past, Robbie had always laughed such stories off but he had finally had enough and decided to go to court. 'Robbie is absolutely livid,' said a friend. 'The story simply isn't true and he is sick of people questioning his sexuality. He's had a laugh in the past about fancying men but that's just Robbie on the wind-up. He is a red-blooded bloke and has been out with a string of stunning women. What more proof is there about his sexuality than that? Robbie is a good bloke and holds his hands up when stories written about him are true. But he is determined to stick up for himself when people spread lies about him.' The joke had clearly gone far enough.

Robbie had also now found a new collaborator, whose identity caused surprise in some quarters. The man in question was Stephen Duffy, who had been in Duran Duran before they became famous. He'd gone on to have a brief solo career before forming the critically acclaimed band The Lilac Time, which was influenced by folk music. The partnership would turn into a stunning success but, at the time, it seemed a daring choice. Stephen was musically very different from Guy Chambers: Robbie was taking a risk.

In October 2004, Robbie made musical history. To accompany the launch of his *Greatest Hits* album, Robbie's record label, EMI, decided to sell mobile-phone memory cards with video content in conjunction with Carphone Warehouse. This meant people with mobile phones could view his latest artistic endeavour on their handsets, with EMI assuring everyone that the sound quality was comparable to a CD. Thus Robbie became the first artist to release an album with video content on a mobile-phone memory card.

The album was a staggering success. It went to No 1 in no fewer than 18 countries, prompting great excitement about the next album, Robbie's first with Stephen Duffy. The pair had 'established a very good writing partnership over the last year', according to Robbie's manager David Enthoven, who added that he had 'been privy to hearing the material and I know how good the songs are'. The pressure was on both Stephen and Robbie – Stephen to prove that he was as good as Guy, and Robbie to prove that he didn't need Guy to be a success.

Robbie was also becoming noted for his appearances in aid of charity. Towards the end of 2004, he joined the ranks of show-business royalty when he took part in a remake of the Band Aid single, 'Do They Know It's Christmas?' Recorded 20 years after the original, it also featured the likes of Sir Paul McCartney, Chris Martin, Dizzee Rascal and Ms Dynamite, and acted as a precursor to the major charitable event in the showbiz calendar, due to take place the following summer: Live 8.

There was widespread agreement afterwards that Robbie had stolen the show. And that was quite a show to steal: his fellow entertainers included Sir Paul McCartney (again), Bob Geldof, Bono, Madonna, Coldplay, Sir Elton John and others too numerous to mention. But Robbie rose above them all: he opened with Queen's 'We Will Rock You', which brought to mind the show-stopper of the previous event, Freddie Mercury, before launching into a string of hits and, finally, in the middle of 'Angels', he went out into the crowd to sing. There was bedlam: the audience lapped it up and Robbie ended as the hero of the day.

A test of a different kind came in November that year with the release of Robbie's latest album, *Intensive Care*, which featured the hit single 'Tripping'. This was the first time his new partnership with Stephen Duffy had been put to the test, and Stephen had certainly given his all. He had co-produced the record, helped to write the songs and played some of the instruments. It was recorded in Robbie's Los Angeles home and, on its release in November 2005, went straight to the top of the UK charts at No 1. The relief all round –

especially at EMI – was palpable. They'd done it: even without Guy Chambers, Robbie was a formidable force.

Finally, as the year drew to a close, came the court case everyone had been waiting for. Robbie went to court over a series of stories that had appeared in a number of papers and magazines in 2004 claiming that he was secretly gay. Robbie had often joked about the rumours that he was more interested in men than women, but he obviously felt these stories had now gone too far, not so much for depicting him as gay as for making him out to be a hypocrite and lying to fans.

In August 2004, the *People* newspaper had published a story with the headline ROBBIE'S SECRET GAY LOVER over an article claiming that he was trying to deceive the public over his sexual orientation at a time when a book about him, *Feel*, was about to be published. Once Robbie's lawyer stood up in court, the gloves were off. 'Mr Williams is not, and never has been, homosexual,' said his counsel, Tom Williams QC. He went on to say that the paper had alleged Robbie was 'pretending' that his only sexual relations had been with women. Robbie won. The case ended with substantial libel damages being awarded, with the various papers and magazines fully accepting that the allegations were false. The rest of Fleet Street had a field day and there was extensive coverage of the case. Famous people's sex lives are a great source of fascination to the British public and this case had had celebrity-watchers agog.

But the whole point was not so much the allegations of homosexuality as those of hypocrisy, something Robbie made clear by his actions. At the time that the piece had appeared, he'd given an extremely good-natured interview to *Attitude*, a gay-lifestyle magazine. The interview was to mark the release of his *Greatest Hits* but it did a good deal more than that: it gave Robbie the chance to make it clear quite how unconcerned he was about being thought to be gay.

He agreed to take part in a regular slot in the magazine called 'How Gay Are You?' designed to test the gayness of the straight subject in question. Robbie went along with it enthusiastically, at one point whipping out a deodorant stick with 'rehydrating moisturiser'. 'How gay is that?' joked Robbie. 'I am very nearly Donatella Versace. That's how gay I am!'

To make the point further, on the day that he won the court case, Robbie turned up on Australian television.

'I'm not gay in Australia,' he announced. 'I'm gay in a lot of places, but not there, for some reason.'

To say his popularity was higher than ever is not overstating the case. Robbie was preparing an 'Intensive Care' tour for 2006 and, in December 2005, it was announced that Robbie would play at Croke Park in Dublin in June. Eighty thousand seats went on sale at 8am and sold out within twenty minutes. The Robster was still on top.

As Robbie's 2006 world tour got under way, he was breaking all records, with tickets selling out almost the moment they were announced. However, his various triumphs couldn't help but be slightly overshadowed by the resurgence of his former colleagues in Take That. The group's comeback had been wildly successful, far more so than anyone had been expecting, but Robbie's absence only served to highlight that some wounds were still very raw.

Robbie himself had made no bones about blaming the band's former manager, Nigel Martin-Smith, for much of his troubles, but now Martin-Smith decided he, too, would speak out. The documentary the previous year had been instrumental in getting the boys together again but Martin-Smith claimed that it had not revealed the whole truth about what had gone on.

'Everything we did was an organic process – we never had a master plan and just went with the flow,' he said. 'When it suddenly ended, I was absolutely devastated. I felt like my right arm had been chopped off. The band had been my life. The documentary was supposed to be the reality of what happened. But it was not. There was so much they didn't show or explain.

'When they asked Robbie why he was so angry with me and why, after ten years, he couldn't forgive me, they didn't show that he stuttered and stammered and hadn't got anything to say. He sees it as all my fault. Robbie has admitted that he took drugs. He said he was sacked and he only took drugs because of me, and the public bought that and so saw him as the underdog. What people don't realise is that Robbie was releasing singles when he left but they were only reaching [UK] No 10. As soon as he came out with his sob story, as the victim of a nasty manager, he started to sell records.

'Robbie said he would have made it without me or Take That. This is not true because, when I took him on, he was seventeen, had puppy fat, was very spoilt, had no father around and was living with his sister and mother, who worshipped him. His auditions were very showbiz, with Mick Jagger impressions.

He wasn't a singer, just a bit of an entertainer. My job was to tighten him up and make him play the game. His mum resented that, as she was very protective, and this affected my relationship with them. The truth is that it took eighteen months to get Robbie to start working. Mark should get the credit for this, as he took him under his wing.'

Robbie's own feelings were still very mixed. He had certainly been reconciled with some former band members, calling Mark 'a genius – the nicest person I've ever met'. He had also publicly (and generously) given credit to Gary, saying, 'You're an amazing songwriter and I apologise for saying that you weren't.'

But that was not the full story. 'I'd go into a room with Mark, Howard and Jason now, but with Gary there's a strange mixture of guilt about what I said and knowing I wouldn't get any resolution,' he said. There was clearly still a great deal to be resolved.

For his part, Gary was clear about what had caused the problems – that Robbie was turning up at rehearsals clearly the worse for wear. 'At one point in the dance sequence, Robbie had to throw Jason backwards, and you're thinking that, if Robbie's not up to that, J could break his neck,' he said. 'That was the point when we said, "Listen, are you going to do these shows or not? We don't want you to go but, if you go now, at least we can get sorted in time." He said, "If you want me to leave, I'll go."'

Mark, Robbie's great mate in the band, was more philosophical, although he, too, had regrets. 'We had to separate,' he said. 'We had spent seven years in one another's pockets. On the day we split, we all got into different cars and went our own ways. It was like hearses taking us to our funerals. I didn't see Gary, Jason or Howard again for three years.

'In the beginning, Rob and I were really close. But by the time the band was coming to an end, there wasn't room for friendship. It was all work and less fun. I felt bad afterwards that we never sat down and talked about it. The day he left was bizarre. We sat chatting in McDonald's, feeling jaded. An hour later, he was gone. I should have phoned him over the weekend. On Monday, I expected him to come back, but he didn't.'

Matters were not helped by the announcement of the nominations for that year's Brit Awards. Robbie only got one nomination, for Best Male Solo Artist, which must have been a disappointment as his most recent album, *Intensive Care*, co-written by him, had been his most successful release to date, selling over two million copies in six weeks alone.

Rather more cheerful news emerged when it was reported that Robbie had bought shares in Port Vale Football Club, the team he had supported all his life. Indeed, as a child, he had lived close to its Hamil Road stadium. 'Although I can't be at the Vale often, my investment is just to say that my heart is still there and I'm a huge supporter,' he said. 'I'm really excited about what we may be able to do with the club in the future.'

So was Bill Bratt, Port Vale's chairman. 'Robbie has supported Port Vale since he was a lad and we are delighted with [the] announcement,' he said. 'I'm extremely pleased and excited that Robbie has invested in the club. It clearly shows that he cares about Port Vale FC and its future. It's now up to the board and all at Port Vale FC to ensure his investment is used wisely in helping to secure the future at the club. It won't make a great deal of difference really because we do set budgets and we abide by those budgets.' Asked if this meant new players, he continued, 'No, not at all... It isn't that that amount of money that will make that amount of difference. It's very, very welcome and it's fantastic news and will lift the profile of the club but it won't alter the way we work.'

Robbie had long dreamed of being a director of

the club. 'My heart strings have definitely been pulled hearing about Port Vale's problems,' he said. 'I've been a Port Vale fan all my life. When I was younger, I was in the Railway Paddock and I used to dream about sitting in the chairman's box.'

There was now a real wistfulness about Robbie when it came to the past. He had joined the Friends Reunited website, posting a notice saying, 'It turned out well for me so far, got the interview at Butlin's and haven't looked back. If you need an entertainer for your children's party, I do magic tricks and everything!' Obviously he was joking but, even so, it was hard to escape the conclusion that he yearned for his younger days, when life was a great deal simpler than now.

But if nothing else, his current lifestyle certainly had its material rewards. Accounts published for Robbie's company, The In Good Company Co Ltd, revealed that the business had enjoyed sales of £15 million up to the end of March 2005, and that Robbie had paid himself £8.9 million in salary and a further £1.9 million in dividends. Much of this was due to the success of his *Greatest Hits* album, which had sold more than six million copies, as well as generating much more in merchandising.

But money could not buy him happiness. His

attitude towards relationships continued to vacillate wildly. One minute he wanted one, the next he was complaining about people calling him a commitment-phobe. 'Look, we could all psychoanalyse Robbie Williams,' he said, while admitting he sometimes went online to find out what people were saying about him. 'I'm not desperate to be in a relationship. It's another piece of the jigsaw, that's all. I'm alone. I'm not lonely. I'm OK. I've got the computer and the sleeping pills. Things are fine. I know people will say, "Check out the ego on Robbie Williams going online to see what people say about him." But it's never anything nice!'

Despite all the old wounds, they had all moved on. Take That were again enormously successful, while Robbie was taking on all the stresses of a five-month tour. It was the longest he'd ever undertaken by himself and it had put a strain on him, as he admitted nearly two months into the tour. 'I've only toured for, at the most, one month at a time when I was in Take That and in my solo career,' he said. 'This tour's five months and I was very concerned that I wasn't going to get through it or that something would happen. I got very scared of the length. But it's easy. I've done two months and I'm still here – two arms, two legs. I've still got a voice. I'm good.'

This time round, he was determined to travel in comfort. He was to tour in a £220,000 customised Winnebago, described by an insider as 'a five-star suite on wheels. It's very impressive. He's got his own bedroom, complete with a king-size bed and an en-suite bathroom with marble sink, bath and shower. There are scented Jo Malone candles throughout. He'll be putting his all into the tour and wants to turn this Winnebago into a real retreat where he can get some time to himself. He's done his time in grotty tour buses and, with more than £70 million in the bank, he reckons he deserves to travel in style.' Indeed, it was luxury on wheels: Italian sofas lined the walls, and it was furnished with a top-of-the-range stereo system. It took the edge off the hard work.

Indeed, the time was whizzing past, with various highlights along the way. 'I can't believe how fast it is actually getting from one gig to another,' he said, recalling one particularly momentous occasion in Milan. 'Italy had just won the World Cup when I got on stage in this huge stadium that looked like the Death Star from *Star Wars* on the outside. The San Siro stadium just carries on for ever and the crowd just doesn't stop. And it was like I'd been invited to their party because they'd won the World Cup.'

Munich was another night that stood out. 'I don't know why it was,' he said. 'I think it was because the weather wasn't so hot. Everywhere else we've been has been really, really hot. But the first night in Munich, it threatened to rain and I think that just gives the crowd more energy because the sun is sapping for me and the crowd. I think I performed the best on the first night, the best I have performed this year. I hope the people who were at that concert that night agree with me.'

He was, however, missing the company of Jonathan Wilkes, who was now happily married. 'There's not a lot of shenanigans, really,' he confessed. 'My best friend on tour would be Jonny and we'd wind people up. There's been no tricks or anything. It's difficult to say whether there's been shenanigans because I'm either in my hotel room or I'm at the venue. You know I can't go out really and sometimes I can't even go to the hotel bar. So there's not been a lot of shenanigans. There's just been a lot of, "Let's watch this movie," or, "Let's do a quiz." Because 1.6 million or 2.8 million people have turned up and bought the tickets, I've got to turn up and give them a good show. It's scary.'

Indeed, Jonathan was now a father, and Robbie was to be the baby's godfather. Nikki, Jonathan's wife, had given birth to Mickey in April, and a thrilled father was happy to take on his new responsibilities. 'Nikki and Mickey are doing great,' said Jonathan after the happy event. 'He was born this morning at seven-twenty [in the morning] and I fainted at seven-twenty-one. We are both so happy and can't wait to get our new family back home. Rob was the first to know about the baby and, of course, he's going to be godfather. He's my best mate.'

Their worlds had clearly diverged: Jonathan was settling into domestic bliss while Robbie was on the road again. But the tour did not go entirely according to plan. A special effect that didn't work on the first night had Robbie offering the bemused audience a refund. In Dublin, he was supposed to be lowered to the stage on a gondola but it failed to work. Ever the showman, Robbie rallied: 'I'm coming back and doing another show for free!' he cried to enthralled fans at Croke Park. 'On my next show, the fucking gondola will work!' By the end of the tour, however, he was plainly exhausted and talking about stopping live performances for good. Nor, to be frank, did it help that everything was going so well for Take That. All the old emotions caused by the initial split had resurfaced and were not easily put away again.

For the first time in years, it seemed as if Robbie's career might not carry on as successfully as up till now. There were worrying signs that, for the first time since he'd left his old band, Robbie was faltering musically. In the summer of 2006, he released a new single, 'Sin, Sin, Sin', the first he had co-written with Stephen Duffy, alongside a video shot in Cape Town. It was a major disappointment in the UK: the first of his singles that didn't get into the Top 20, peaking at UK No 22. It did, however, do better in Europe and Latin America.

A slightly happier experience had been with Matt Lucas of *Little Britain*, who had been staying at Robbie's LA mansion when Robbie was struggling to find the right lyrics for a song. Matt stepped into the role. 'The track worked out brilliantly,' said a friend. 'Robbie wasn't happy with this song's lyrics, so he just asked Matt if he had any ideas. He came up with some words about a bloke with OCD [obsessive compulsive disorder] who wants to go out on a date but whose condition stops him leaving the house. Matt was too nervous to sing in front of Robbie, so he waited until Robbie went off to play football and then recorded his vocals alone.'

But it was an isolated patch in a difficult time. Robbie himself seemed to be voicing doubts about the future. He had, after all, been doing this for a long time now and was showing clear signs of wanting to have a break. 'I've got to take the view over the next eighteen months and see if I want to be part of the machine, because I don't see me singing again,' he said. 'It's a question of what I want and where I want to be. Can I live without radio picking my song and putting it on the playlist? Or is this fame thing something I'm addicted to? I don't know where I stand with it all at the moment. Do I take things into my own hands and dismantle this monster and have a nice life?' He might not have been being entirely serious – everyone has moments of self-doubt – but he was clearly in a quandary.

Nor were matters helped with the release of *Rudebox*, Robbie's seventh album, in the autumn. It was widely considered to be a dud compared with his past work and a spectacularly badly timed dud at that. The reviews did not make for cheering reading. One magazine said, 'What a bizarre, baffling and downright strange record this is.' Another newspaper fretted over 'an album so peculiar, so spectacularly misconceived, that it will decimate his fan base at a stroke'.

Rudebox marked a departure from his usual style, as it ventured into the field of dance music.

The title track was released as a single, prompting yet more harsh words from the critics. 'Robbie Williams' new track, "Rudebox", is not only the worst song by him I've heard, it's the worst record I've ever heard,' said one typical review. Another critic asked, 'When was the last time there was a really good Robbie Williams record?' It was not Robbie's finest hour and the single did not go down well with his fans.

Robbie was still very much the ladies' man, however, and managed to fit in a brief romance with Tara Palmer-Tomkinson – something she herself inadvertently made public. 'I was a bit excited so I told somebody – well, you would, wouldn't you?' she said to Terry Wogan. 'I'm only human. I was like, "It's Robbie Williams!" The next thing I see, it's all over a magazine. I really learned from that mistake. The problem is, if you talk about relationships that you're having, the relationship goes out of the window. I can't tell you because it would all be over. But Robbie's great, that's the main thing.' It didn't last long but the two remained friends.

His relationships stood in marked contrast to his professional career. The world outside had noticed the divergence between Robbie's fortunes and those of his former bandmates, and it was only too happy to speculate that there must be serious problems behind the scenes.

CHAPTER SIX

ROBBIE'S TRAVAILS

Robbie finally seemed to be giving up on the idea of cracking America. *Rudebox* had had a bad enough reception in Britain: he clearly didn't want to repeat the experience over there. 'They're not having it,' he said to Capital FM DJ Johnny Vaughan. 'I'm not releasing it there. The only way an album of mine is going to be in the States is if I leave it there or leave it in Tower Records. I'll go with a bunch and just leave them.'

Nor did he seem able to stay away from the area that had caused so much trouble in the past – his sexuality. The subject of gay sex came up yet again when Robbie speculated on what could make him have sex with a man: 'I wouldn't enjoy it but I could do it under pain of death, or if it meant saving a baby bunny from being burned alive.' Robbie appeared to be as obsessed with the idea as ever.

It surfaced again when Robbie responded to comments made by Louis Walsh, the *X Factor* judge, to the effect that Robbie's voice was not 'all that...' Robbie was hurt, especially as the two of them had been friends in the old days. 'Louis has started slagging me off all the time,' said Robbie. 'I didn't have any history with him so I don't know why he's doing it. He should decide if he wants to be a manager or a celebrity – I don't think you can be both.'

The winner of the *X Factor* that year was Shayne Ward, and Robbie was keen to offer friendship to him, giving him his phone number and telling him to call. Shayne didn't, something Robbie also put down to Louis Walsh. 'I phone in and vote – it becomes the most important thing in your life at that moment,' he said. 'I voted for three or four people on the last *X Factor*, including Shayne Ward and the dustbin man, Andy.'

The fling with Tara Palmer-Tomkinson now over, Robbie was also back looking for love. Katie Melua revealed that he had been pursuing her, having called her management company to get her number but, despite thinking him 'lovely', she had turned him down. 'I don't think I could see myself with someone who's famous,' she said. 'I don't like the lifestyle and everything it stands for. Too superficial. That attention is too much. For me to go home and be surrounded by that sounds like a fucking nightmare. But a musician or someone who's into music is different.'

With all this going on, it was not really a surprise when Robbie turned up in a TV documentary made by Stephen Fry, *The Secret Life of the Manic Depressive*. Robbie was having increasing problems with depression, which were becoming public and here, along with the likes of actress Carrie Fisher, actor-comedian Tony Slattery and chef Rick Stein, he discussed the problem as it affected him. What was clear, however, was that his manic behaviour on stage was due to showmanship, not depression. Robbie might have had his problems off the stage, but on it he was still capable of giving his all. The depression had surfaced just over a year after he gave up drinking; his addiction, he said, was to 'fantasy'.

However, this new batch of problems did take its toll. He was reported to be seeing Dr Mark Collins, a psychiatrist at The Priory, as he struggled with a new bout of depression. He also got caught up in a bizarre feud with Rod Stewart's stepson Ashley Hamilton, arguing over ownership of a song they had worked on together. He was said to have called him frequently, using strong language, outraged that Ashley had gone public over the spat. Observers who were used to Robbie's strange behaviour were becoming concerned: Robbie had been through very difficult patches before and seemed to be heading that way again.

He was still keen on mooning, too: in October 2006, he won Best International Act award at the MTV Latin American Awards in Mexico City, something he celebrated by dropping his trousers before enthusiastically kissing a very pretty fan.

But a longer-term relationship continued to elude him, something that Robbie seemed increasingly to accept. 'I don't know if I want to be in a relationship,' he said. 'I don't believe that to be fulfilled you have to have kids. What's the point? I can't guarantee my child won't suffer pain – because that kid's going to be in pain at some point in their life. I don't want to see that. It's too much.'

There were other problems about settling down, too. Robbie, after all, rather enjoyed the single life, and the thought of having to give it up was not that appealing. 'I won't be fit to marry for another ten years – just look at my life,' he said. 'For the first two or three years of my sobriety, I was desperate to be in a relationship because I thought it would fix me. But if you're in a relationship, you have to keep your dick in your pants – and I'd struggle with that. Now I don't want a relationship. I look at them and think, "What's in it for me?"'

Indeed, he said he understood George Michael's nocturnal adventures. 'If there was a wood near my house full of women who wanted to have sex, I'd find it difficult not to go there,' he said.

Nor was the struggle to stay sober any easier than it had been. 'I hate drugs, I love drugs,' he said. 'They haven't invented a new one that's not bad for you or less depressing than ecstasy, or one that makes you less paranoid than coke. As depressing as it is, as soul-destroying, relationship-destroying as it is, it makes life fucking interesting.'

The touring was beginning to take its toll, too. There were increasing reports that Robbie was exhausted, which were confirmed when the Far Eastern leg of the tour, due to start in November, was cancelled. Elton John spoke publicly about his concerns: 'Robbie is the number-one star in the world,' he said. 'He should let the other shit go and, if he can't, he needs to see someone and talk about it. All he is doing is burning a hole inside of himself, eating him up, making him angry and miserable.'

The people around him on tour were worried, too. 'The past few weeks before we arrived back in Britain have been pretty awful,' said one. 'Some days, Rob has been sleeping till three [in the afternoon], then saying he can't go on stage that night. The tour is draining for everyone, but particularly for Rob, and he has not looked at all happy. In the end, the only thing to do was to cancel the Far East section. Some pretty terrified promoters from South America and Australia are desperate to know if their tours will be next to go.'

In the event, most of the scheduled tours did go ahead, but problems kept recurring. There was an outcry in September when Robbie played Roundhay Park in Leeds and the local council decided to shut 11 schools for the day or close them early because of the traffic chaos expected before the concert. Robbie was in no way to blame for this but still came in for criticism on the grounds that he was harming children's education. Mark Harris, leader of Leeds City Council, stepped up to take the rap.

'Certainly on the schools issue, we did not think it through and we should have done,' he said. 'It was not made clear to the schools early enough that there were going to have to be significant road closures and these schools were going to have to close. I am not the sort of politician who would try to give some mealy mouthed answer to insult the public, who can clearly see what has happened.'

Meanwhile, the newly reformed Take That were now well and truly on the way up. In November 2006, they released 'Patience', their first single for ten years, which sold more than 20,000 copies on the day of its release. '"Patience" is well on its way to giving the band their ninth UK No 1,' said a delighted Gennaro Castaldo, spokesman for HMV. 'It also makes them early contenders to top the singles chart this Christmas.' Indeed, they went on to do just that. Robbie had no comment to make on the subject, publicly at least, but it can't have been easy for him: every triumph for Take That was publicly interpreted as a direct snub for him.

In fact, he didn't have that much to be worried about. It might seem a strange way to judge someone's personality but the world of show business is not like other worlds, so Robbie could comfort himself with the news that his 2007 tour was outselling everyone else's. There were also reports that he'd been in talks with one of the most popular bands of all time, ABBA, about recording one of their songs. 'Robbie and I talked about doing an ABBA hit together,' said Anni-Frid Lyngstad, the brunette singer with the band. 'He has not yet come back on that one.'

Indeed, Robbie was getting support from all over the world. In December, he got into trouble on stage in Australia when he lit up on the stage of a non-smoking theatre, telling the audience it was the only vice he had left. He also informed them he was not a role model. He was fined £120 for lighting the cigarette but was defended by none other than Peter Beattie, the leader of Australia's Queensland state. 'I'll be paying the fines myself because I don't want to see this turned into an opportunity to continue to promote that bad-boy image,' he said. 'He is a guest of Queensland. He came here, entertained a lot of Queenslanders and put a lot of money into the Queensland economy.'

And so 2006 came to an end, a turbulent year for Robbie. Take That were once more at the top of the charts, but this time without him. Critics were only too happy to contrast his own fortunes with those of his former bandmates. Meanwhile, he had suffered a rare flop and was looking unsure about where to go next. But despite any personal and professional setbacks, Robbie remained a wildly popular performer with a huge following worldwide. Still only 32, and with all manner of options open to him, Robbie still had a long way to go and, tantalisingly, there was still the prospect of a reunion with his old bandmates. The following year was to prove more eventful still.

It should have been one of the happiest days of the year. The date was 13 February 2007, Robbie's 33rd birthday. But far from celebrating the occasion, Robbie had booked himself into a rehab clinic in Los Angeles, where he was being treated for an addiction to what was thought to be anti-depressants. 'Robbie has been admitted into a treatment centre for his dependency on prescription drugs,' said his spokesman, Bryony Watts.

It was no secret that Robbie had suffered from similar problems in the past. In the documentary *The Secret Life of the Manic Depressive*, he had been quite open about it. 'My first drug of choice was probably fantasy – fantasising about being an actor or being a singer or going to the moon,' he'd said. 'I don't know if that was to escape the depression. I was sad that my career was going up and my self-esteem was going down. With me, how my depression manifested itself was that I would stop going out. I would get up in front of forty-thousand people and say, "Look at me, I'm ace." Then as soon as I got off stage, I would go back to my bedroom and pull the duvet over my eyes. Cocaine gave me a twitch and drink just made me ill – so all the props I had just had to be removed.'

He was clearly prone to these episodes, and the past year hadn't helped. The comparisons with Take That, who were going from strength to strength, continued to be made, and this time it was not Robbie who was coming out on top. The quartet was set to clean up at the forthcoming Brit Awards but Robbie had only one nomination. Then there were the very real strains of being in his position. It is easy, not least because of his wealth, to dismiss the problems of being in the public eye but Robbie was constantly under observation. Everything he said or did made the news and that caused a strain.

'He has a vulnerable side and is very human,' said his sister Sally. 'People tend to put him on a pedestal and he has almost become public property. There is a lot of pressure that goes with that. He has a good family. Our mother has been fantastic and is incredibly supportive. She has done an awful lot for us both. Our thoughts are with him. We love him and we are there to support him.'

The clinic he was being treated at was located in the Arizona desert, and Robbie was to stay for three weeks at a cost of £20,000. His mother Jan was highly relieved at his decision. 'I have known about Robbie's problems for some time and it has been very worrying,' she said. 'But from a mother's point of view, going into rehab is the best gift he could have given himself.'

In time, it emerged that Robbie had become hooked on the anti-depressants Seroxat and Xanax, as well as the painkiller Vicodin. He was also on 60 cigarettes, 20 Red Bulls and 36 double espressos a day – enough to put anyone's system into burnout. 'I can't honestly say that I don't take too many prescription drugs,' he confessed in one interview. 'How many is too many? If you drink as much coffee as I do, you easily get into the too-many-sleeping-tablets thing.'

Indeed, it soon became clear that Robbie really needed help. He had had a two-month relationship with the American model Lisa D'Amato and she gave some insight into what his life had become, revealing that he was a bag of nerves, even in his sleep. 'He'd shake uncontrollably, looking like a frightened child,' she said. 'He's so tormented. When he started shaking, I would gently lift him into my arms and rub his arms and legs until he stopped. He didn't wake up but it seemed to calm him down.'

She, too, related that Robbie spent hours logged on to the internet to find out what people were saying about him, and that he hated being on stage. 'It was clear he was struggling with his mind,' she said. 'He doesn't need drink but he needs anti-depressants to get him through the day. A lot of the time, he seemed on edge. He would light up a cigarette then put it out and light another straight away.'

It was remarked upon in some quarters that Robbie's spell in rehab coincided with the Brits at which, as predicted, Take That reigned supreme, winning Best Single. Robbie had been nominated for Best Live Act but didn't win. It was also remarked upon that the boys did not mention Robbie in their speeches – although, after what he'd said about them and given that they'd made the comeback on their own, there was no reason they should have done. At any rate, Gary was keen to emphasise afterwards that there had been no deliberate snub. 'There are some people who will never be happy and I fear that Robbie will be one of them,' he said. 'We haven't heard from him in ages and the boys and I hope that he is OK.'

That was not the only time the subject of Robbie came up during the awards. The host for the night was Russell Brand, who got into trouble because of the risky nature of the jokes was telling. One fairly mild example was when he pointed to a giant padlock on the stage and quipped, 'Robbie Williams' medicine cabinet.' 'Let me entertain you, as long as you don't need twenty Red Bulls and sixty fags to do it,' he continued, urging the audience to send their love to Robbie. 'He's a favourite of the Brits,' he went on. 'Get well, England's Rose. Curse them drugs, they're evil.' Perhaps it was fortunate that Robbie wasn't there.

Gary Barlow certainly thought so. Robbie failed to win the award he'd been up for, which some cynics believed explained his absence. Gary, despite the goodwill he was expressing towards his old bandmate, appeared to be one of them. 'If I was doing rehab, you would never know,' he said. 'But a press release giving all the reasons why... What a coincidence!'

Liam Gallagher thought so, too, and said so, a lot more loudly. 'If you ask me, it's fucking suspicious. He gets himself on all the fucking front pages on that day, going into rehab, so everyone's going, "Ah, poor, poor fucking Robbie, how fucking sad,"' he said. 'And if he hadn't gone into rehab, everyone would have been going, "Oh look, Robbie's got fuck-all at the Brits and his album was shit and no one gives a fuck about him any more."'

Nigel Martin-Smith was similarly sniffy. 'This is typical of Robbie,' he said. 'He's very theatrical. His whole life is one huge soap opera. He might be after a bit of sympathy. If I was a Robbie fan, I wouldn't be worried. He'll go to his rehab, have a lie down and a couple of Anadins and he'll be fine.' Sympathetic it wasn't, but then that was hardly to be expected. There was no love lost between Robbie and Nigel, and neither would have been prepared to take a gentler stand.

But Robbie did have problems and no one was more aware of that than his mother. 'There was one time when he came home in the middle of his drink-and-drug problems,' Jan revealed to *Staffordshire County* magazine. 'He lay down on the rug with his head in my lap and I looked down at him and he was sobbing. For a moment, I felt I was looking into a mirror, like it was my reflection. As a mother, it was mind blowing. I reacted as a mother first and foremost, and stuck to him like glue. There was a lot of trauma.

'It's very, very hard when your child has problems. Alcohol and drugs don't just affect the person who takes them. But as bad as some of it has been with

Robert – and some of it has been a living hell – there have always been lots of lovely things. He has to make his own choices and I have to let go. He's thirty-three and says to me, "I'm a big boy, don't worry." But as a mother, you do. I worry he's exhausted after that tour he did last year. Take a sixteen-year-old, put him in the music industry and what emerges is someone with plenty of scars.

'What would I like for him in the next ten years? He has said he'd like a family and I'd like more grandchildren. I know what I'd like for him but it's his life. A lot of people around him have got married and had babies but it's difficult in the industry he's in. A tour like last year's takes twelve months, with twelve months' preparation. There isn't much room to do normal things.'

Robbie was still in rehab when he won another award – one he certainly wouldn't have wanted: Worst Album for *Rudebox* at the NME Awards. His old foe Noel Gallagher – who had won a Lifetime Achievement award at the Brits – was present and not slow to gloat. 'I just wish he was here so I could say, "Well done,"' he said. 'I don't think even Robbie himself thinks he's a credible artist. I could talk to you for three hours about how bad he is. Worst Album isn't really an award, is it?'

At least he still had a friend in Mark Owen, who was showing genuine concern at the state Robbie was in. 'When I heard about him checking into rehab, I felt sad – I just want him to be happy again,' he said. 'I'll do anything I can to help him. If he wants me to see him, I'll be straight on that plane. Me and Rob went through a period when we didn't speak, but then he got in touch. Rob was always my mate. I'm so worried about him.'

Some people thought his old songwriting partner Guy Chambers might be able to help although, given Robbie's sensitivity about his fortunes after parting from Guy, that might have been a bit too close to home. In any event, Guy was not sure he'd be of any use. 'The idea was to get Guy on board to try to help Robbie lift his spirits a bit with a friendly voice from home,' said a source. 'He has been so fragile lately. But Guy was really surprised to be contacted out of the blue. He hadn't spoken to Robbie for ages and didn't see how he could help. Robbie and Guy used to be so close but their friendship soured. They have been in touch periodically since their fall-out but their relationship is nothing like it once was.'

EMI would certainly have been delighted to have seen a reconciliation between the two. Having spent such a huge amount in signing Robbie up, they needed to see a decent return on their investment and *Rudebox* wasn't it. 'If Chambers was to appear back on the scene in a songwriting capacity, we would be jubilant,' said a source at the label. 'Robbie isn't very popular at the moment as he was warned *Rudebox* might bomb. But he is seen as a cash cow and it's imperative to EMI that he gets back on track. Everybody is concerned he's in a clinic, but it's a step in the right direction.'

In the event, Robbie stayed at the clinic until 7 March 2007, at which point his mother Jan went to the US to look after him. 'Robbie Williams has completed his stay in Arizona and is continuing with an after-care programme in Los Angeles,' said his spokeswoman. His stay, however, had been a fortnight shorter than expected, leading to rumours that Robbie couldn't take the tough regime. His sister Sally denied this. 'He didn't leave the clinic because he couldn't handle it,' she said. 'There was an issue between staff and a patient that he wasn't happy with, so he decided to continue his treatment elsewhere. He needs to get to a place where he feels happy with his own life before he can even start thinking about coming back.'

His father, Pete Conway, was pleased about the way the treatment had progressed. 'I always know how Robbie is by his humour, and it's back,' he said just after Robbie had got out. 'He was making jokes down the phone to me yesterday. They are not quotable – very private and a bit rude. So I would say he is on the mend. He's not going back to rehab – he's done, he's finished. I am looking forward to seeing him more than you could know. I always have faith in him – he's a good lad and I love him.'

Robbie certainly seemed in fighting form. The day after leaving the clinic, he went to a meeting with the Rock & Republic store in Culver City, California, sparking speculation that he might be signing a deal to do a clothing line. The company had a number of celebrity designers on its books, including Victoria Beckham. He also stepped straight back into the social whirl. Two nights in a row, he was seen out at nightclubs, staying sober and clearly enjoying himself. 'He seemed on good form,' said an onlooker. 'He looked incredibly smart as he left the club with a group of his friends and I think he really enjoyed himself. It is good to see him looking so fresh faced.'

His time in rehab had given Robbie the chance to mull over recent events and it now emerged that he, too, had decided that *Rudebox* was a mistake. 'Well, this is the thing,' he said. 'I absolutely, positively know that I'm not a rapper. I'm not. I'd love to be but I'm me – I come from Take That! I believe everyone is saying, "Robbie can't rap." Yeah, I can't, but I'm not rapping. For me, it's about having more bars in a song and, therefore, more words, more pictures painted. Mike Skinner's not a rapper.'

He compounded this by revealing that he had tried to work with the hip-hop producer Timbaland, to no avail. 'I tried to get in touch with Timbaland but there was no joy back from anybody,' he said, adding that he'd also tried to contact the British rapper Sway, with negative results. 'I was so disappointed, 'cause fuck what you think of me but, just as a human being to another human being, I sent him an email going, "I really fucking love this, mate – it's dead funny, dead clever, it's really on it."' Robbie said.

His time in rehab also brought home another message: money does not necessarily mean happiness. 'I'm blessed to know that it hasn't bought me happiness,' he said. 'I've had to look elsewhere for that happiness and I've got it, but it's a difficult one to talk about. I've been thinking a lot about when I did the record-signing for the contract. I remember saying, "I'm rich beyond my wildest dreams." It was an absolutely stupid thing to say out loud. I've been thinking about that the last couple of days. It's the most embarrassing thing I've ever done.'

Meanwhile, Take That continued with one success after another and still Robbie's career appeared to falter. Their second single, 'Shine', made it to UK No 1, while Robbie's latest, 'She's Madonna', made in collaboration with the Pet Shop Boys, only made it to UK No 16. This was not what Robbie was used to. He was the man who had landed the biggest record deal in history, who had made the *Guinness Book of Records* for the speed at which his concerts had sold out and who was adored across the globe.

But Robbie rallied. He was seen out on the town in LA – indeed, he was seen out and about so much that some people began to worry it would impede his recovery. Then he was spotted in the company of wild-child actress Lindsay Lohan, who had also just completed a stint in rehab, leading to speculation that there might be more than friendship between the pair. In the event, however, nothing more came of it.

Curiously, Melanie Chisholm, aka Sporty Spice, aka Mel C, chose this moment to clear up the rumours that she and Robbie had once had a relationship. She did so with typical gusto. 'I've turned down so many people on this question,' she said. 'It was ten fucking years ago and I'm still talking about it! It was nothing serious but we went on a couple of dates and it didn't really work out. It was just a chemistry thing, really: sometimes there's not a major reason. He was busy travelling all over the world and so was I. At the end of the day, you're never going to get Robbie to settle down, are you? You're never going to tame that beast!'

She was, however, very sympathetic about his recent problems. 'I felt for him when he went to rehab,' she said. 'Robbie will have to deal with his demons for ever, especially with something like addiction. I'm not comparing myself to Robbie in any way, but I hope and pray that I wouldn't get depressed if my album didn't do well. I try really hard to get a balance in my life so that my career isn't the only thing in it.'

What was of greater interest, however, was Robbie's relationship with Take That. The boys had been extremely generous about their old friend turned tormentor, openly urging him to rejoin the band. Gary was constantly saying nice things about him, while Jason commented, 'Maybe it's my romanticism but, I think if we do future albums, it's inevitable Rob will sing with us.'

Someone very close to Robbie agreed – his mother Jan. 'He's thrilled at how Take That have come back,' she said. 'On the question of him doing something with them, I feel that will happen. It would be something he wanted to do. I'm thrilled out of all the negative stuff that happened in the past, there's now something great happening.' Robbie's recovery was also going well. 'He's enjoying his life and his football and going out with the lads,' she said. 'He's writing and spends a lot of time in the studio.'

Of course, a reunion was not going to be plain sailing. A lot of insults had been traded over the years and everyone involved was going to have to be pretty mature about getting back together – not a given, considering some of the people involved. Indeed, Gary Barlow admitted as much. 'I mean, he said some horrible things about me, but I'm old enough to get over that now,' he said. 'I think that's the beauty of having kids, as well – it teaches you that there are things in life that just aren't important.'

But he was extremely generous about Robbie, too, crediting their old bandmate's solo success with giving them all a second chance. 'If I'm really, really honest, we wouldn't have had a chance to be Take That again if it wasn't for him still being a successful artist,' he said. 'We met him while on tour and I exchange emails. A couple of the guys get texts from him and we're on a really good note with him. We're at an age when there's no point [in feuding] – there's enough trouble in the world.'

Would the reunion ever happen? Take That themselves were split. 'I really want him to,' said Jason, while Take That was touring Australia. 'I think it would be good for him, for us and for Take That.'

Howard disagreed. 'I think it could be a big mistake,' he said. 'We don't know Robbie. Even though Jason calls him or Gary might email him, we don't know him – we really don't.' Clearly, there was still some way to go.

For now, Robbie kept himself out of sight. The touring stopped, the feuding abated and he contented himself with some of his more eccentric interests, such as spotting UFOs. His life changed completely when he met Ayda Field in 2007; the couple would marry three years later. Robbie had finally found fulfilment in his personal life, and he was finding his way back to the band with which he had made his name. Everything really had changed.

CHAPTER SEVEN

BACK TO THE BEGINNING

But who, exactly, were these bandmates that Robbie was edging closer to rejoining? And how had they come together to form Take That?

The undisputed leader of Take That, in both its first and second incarnations, is Gary Barlow. Born on 20 January 1970 to Marge and Colin in Frodsham, Cheshire, Gary has one older brother, Ian, and was something of a musical prodigy. Gary attended Weaver Vale school in Frodsham: like Robbie, he was an enthusiastic performer in school plays, taking the role of Joseph in *Joseph and the Amazing Technicolor Dreamcoat*. Gary recalled that he used to love watching *Top of the Pops* on television and that it was Depeche Mode's 'Just Can't Get Enough' that inspired him to learn to play the keyboards.

Indeed, music had Gary in its thrall. At the age of ten, his parents told him he could have either a BMX bike or a keyboard for Christmas: Gary went for the keyboard. 'Within two weeks, I'd done everything on the keyboard and Dad had to buy me a better one,' Gary said in a 1991 interview. It was money well spent. Even at that tender age, he was a regular performer at the Connah's Quay Labour Club in north Wales: he would play gigs on Saturday nights, for which he was paid £18. Two years later, he made the acquaintance of a singer, Heather, and the two started touring locally. With this background, it was almost certain that Gary would soon be following a professional musical career.

But he still needed to pursue some education, so he went on to Frodsham High School, eventually leaving with six O-levels. This was a considerably better academic performance than Robbie's but, even so, Gary's music had pride of place. By the age of 14, he'd found another regular gig, this time at the Halton British Legion near Runcorn. He would play four times every weekend, finishing at about 2am, and it was beginning to bring in some money. At this stage, Gary was earning about £140 a week.

Matters went up to a new level the following year. BBC Pebble Mill was running a competition called

'A Song for Christmas': Gary wrote a song called 'Let's Pray for Christmas' and asked his mother and music teacher, Mrs Nelson, to tell him what they thought. The former didn't like it ('too slow') but the latter did and entered it in to the competition. After several silent weeks, Mrs Nelson heard back from them and had to go and find young Gary in the gym: Pebble Mill wanted Gary to go to the West Heath Studios to record the number, his first ever visit to a studio. He was still only 15.

In the event, the song didn't make it past the semi-finals, but it opened several doors. For a start, Gary met Bob Howes, the songwriting partner of keyboard player Rod Argent, who'd written hits for The Zombies and Argent. Both provided advice and help in the early years. Secondly, and perhaps more importantly, when Gary was invited to Strawberry Studios in Stockport as part of the prize for getting to the semi-finals, he met Mark Owen, who was working there as a tea boy at the weekends. The two went on to form a band together, The Cutest Rush – in other words, the beginnings of Take That.

Mark, born on 27 January 1972, was a little bit younger than Gary. He came from Oldham in Lancashire, from quite a humble background. His father, Keith, was a decorator, who went on to get a job in a police office, while his mother, Mary, was a supervisor in a bakery. Mark has a brother, Daniel, and a sister, Tracy, and the family grew up in a small council house: the three siblings had to share a bedroom.

As a young child, Mark was very keen on doing his Elvis impersonations and, like Gary and Robbie, he later took part in school plays (at St Augustine's Catholic School; his primary school had been Holy Rosary Primary). But back then, he wasn't interested in a career in show business – he wanted to be a footballer. On one occasion, as a young child, Mark was playing football in the alley behind his parents' house when he smashed a window with the ball: worried about what his parents would do when they found out, Mark tried to repair the damage himself. He bought a new pane of glass and was subsequently discovered, hard at work, covered in blood.

Mark left school with six GCSEs and took a job in a local clothes shop, Zuttis. He then worked for a time in a bank. But a footballing career was a real possibility and Mark went on to play for Chadderton FC, a semi-professional club in greater Manchester. He showed real promise and had trials for Manchester United, Huddersfield Town and Rochdale, but an injury to his groin brought his nascent career on the field to a halt.

Initially, Mark was devastated, but his meeting with Gary was to prove his salvation. 'I was fourteen,' he later recalled, 'looking for work as a session singer and Gary was this genius keyboard player.' The two had a modest success with The Cutest Rush but Gary was already setting his sights on the big time. He hired a photographer, Michael Braham, to take publicity shots: it was a fortuitous move. Braham was also working for an entrepreneur called Nigel Martin-Smith.

Across Lancashire, in Droylsden, Howard Paul Donald was born on 28 April 1968, to Keith and Kathleen. He was one of five children: his brothers are Michael, Colin (both older than him) and Glenn (younger), and he has a younger sister, Samantha. Keith and Kathleen separated when Howard was eight, but both had interests that were to prove a profound influence on their son: Keith taught Latin-American dancing and Kathleen had been a singer.

Howard attended Moorside Junior High School in Manchester, and then went on to Little Moss High School for boys, leaving with passes in English, Maths and Geography. His hobbies as a child were riding his BMX bike and breakdancing, but his initial ambition was to be a pilot. However, his first job was very different indeed: on leaving school, Howard went to serve an apprenticeship at the coach-builder Knibbs in Manchester, after which he got a job spraying cars at Wimpole Garages.

But Howard's passion remained breakdancing, which he continued in his spare time. He joined a number of dance groups, including RDS Royal and J and D Dance Troupe, which performed all around Manchester, most notably at the Apollo. They did well: J and D Dance Troupe won first prize three times in a year in the 'Come Dancing' tournament, got to second place in the European championships and third place in the World Breakdancing Championship.

Another member of J and D Dance Troupe was Jason Thomson Orange. Like Howard, he hadn't started out in music, either. Born on 10 July 1970 in Crumpsall, Manchester to Tony and Jenny, he is part of a large family. He has a twin, Justin, and his other siblings are Simon, Dominic, Samuel and Oliver. He also has two half-sisters, Emma and Amy, a stepbrother, Simon, and a stepsister, Sarah. Jason comes from a family of Mormons, who do not believe in drinking coffee or alcohol and live by very strict rules.

Jason first attended Haveley Hey primary school in Wythenshawe, Manchester, after which he went to South Manchester High School, leaving (like Robbie) with no qualifications. A sporty boy, Jason was keen on football, running and swimming, and by his own account, leaving school was a great relief. He walked out of the gates, he said, turned back and thought, "Freedom!"

A career in show business took its time beckoning. Jason and his twin both ended up on a Youth Training Scheme, after which Jason worked as a painter and decorator for Direct Works. But he, too, had discovered the joys of breakdancing and proved so good at it that he began to stand out. He joined the group Street Machine and appeared on the TV show *The Hitman and Her*, presented by Pete Waterman and Michaela Strachan, before he met his future bandmate. Howard and Jason got on and left to form their own breakdancing group, Street Beat.

It was at this point that all of them made the fortuitous acquaintance of Nigel Martin-Smith. He had also left school at 15 with no qualifications and, in June 1981, launched a modelling and casting agency, which by 1990, had grown to employ ten staff and have a £1 million annual turnover. He worked in an office in Manchester's Royal Exchange and was determined to challenge the 'London-centric' attitude of much of show business. He'd dabbled in the music industry before putting together Take That, and had some success with local artist Damian, who had a Top Ten hit in 1989 with a cover of 'The Time Warp'. In addition to that, he ran a Film Artist Agency at Manchester's Half Moon Chambers.

But it was with Take That that Martin-Smith would really make his mark. The American boy band New Kids on the Block had been a massive success and he saw an opportunity for a British version. At the time Gary was 19, Mark 18, Jason, 19 and Howard a relatively ancient 21. Robbie, who was 16 when the band was formed, was the youngest of the lot.

Some years later, Gary recalled where he was when he got the call from Martin-Smith confirming that he would be in the new band. 'I was out the front, washing my car, a Ford Orion,' he recalled. 'You could fit the speaker for my keyboard in the back seat. [Martin-Smith had] an idea for a band ... the comradeship between five nice young people.' He showed Gary a video of New Kids on the Block but Gary fretted that he couldn't dance. He was told not to worry: the band would be built around him. He would be the singer in the middle and the others would work around him.

Jason and Howard were doing well. Street Beat had made the finals of the 'Come Dancing' tournament three times and won twice. They were placed second in the European championships and third in the world for a dance version of *Seven Brides for Seven Brothers*. Howard, fortuitously, signed on as a male model with Martin-Smith, who soon discovered he was a very talented dancer and had a dance partner, Jason. It all began to come together. Howard and Jason's involvement had a direct impact on the way the band came across. 'We all agreed on a sexy image, like the bare chests, coloured waistcoats and beads,' Howard said, 'but with the dancing, I try to keep it tight, so it appeals to both the older and the teenage market.'

And so this, initially, was the line-up of Take That. Gary gave up his club jobs and sold his car. 'We all had jobs we jacked in,' he later said. 'Jason, painting and decorating. Howard, car spraying. Mark was a tea boy at Strawberry Studios. Our manager put us on a little wage and kept us all hyped up. I remember saying to Jason, "One day we're going to be coming in and talking to each other about the houses we've bought and the cars we've bought and the watches we've bought." We laugh about that moment, because that's exactly what we do.'

It was at this point that Robbie was brought in. The others were surprised but they all got on well soon enough. Rehearsals began and the group made their first television appearance on *The Hitman and Her* in 1990, where they performed 'Love' and 'My Kind of Girl'. They then appeared a second time to perform 'Waiting Around', which became the b-side of 'Do What U Like', their first single. They had two releases, 'Promises' and 'Once You've Tasted Love', before they really began to get anywhere.

It was when the band began to make a real effort to cultivate their teen fanbase that it all finally took off. The glory days of Take That first time around were from 1993 to 1995 and what really kick-started it was the release of their second album, *Everything Changes*. The band got four UK No 1 singles from it – 'Pray', 'Relight My Fire', 'Babe' and 'Everything Changes' – and a UK No 3, 'Love Ain't Here Any More'.

Young girls loved them, absolutely loved them. Aware of the importance of each fan being able to fantasise that one day she, too, would go out with a member of Take That, Martin-Smith very publicly imposed a ban on girlfriends, although he did permit quick flings. (Had he not, he would almost certainly have had a revolt on his hands. These were young, attractive men with half the teenagers in the country after them. You couldn't have expected more.)

Although Take That had an extremely clean-living image, behind the scenes it was very different. Robbie's own peccadilloes are well known but, a few years after the break-up, many were still shocked when Gary gave a very revealing interview about what life was really like in the band. 'I've taken cocaine and ecstasy and smoked dope,' he admitted. 'It was wild in Take That and every situation we were in, we did it to the max. I've done drugs but never had a problem. The problem was, if I took E, I'd feel like shit for a week and I just couldn't work. That's why I knocked it on the head. Everyone thought we were saints in Take That. I'm glad I tried them, but I got it out of my system when I was young.

'Drugs and pop stars don't really go together. I'd be so embarrassed if I ever took as much cocaine as Robbie has done. I'd be upset for my parents and so ashamed. For Robbie, it was inevitable. He was like a kid in a sweet shop. I don't know why he fell for it. I've got no respect for that. People like that are on the road to ruin. He seems to like doing things that destroy him.

On our last tour, at rehearsals, he couldn't function. He was doing so many drugs and was in a right old state, like a time bomb. I always remind myself that my life's like I've won the lottery ten times – I don't want to risk wrecking that. I slept with hundreds of girl fans all over the world. But I've got all that out of my system now.'

Not that any of this was evident back then. As the boys toured the UK and Europe, appearing all over the place at such shows as the Brits and *Top of the Pops*, a very lucrative sideline of income came in through merchandising. The boys' faces were not just on the cover of every magazine going: they were on books, stickers, jewellery, dolls, caps, posters, toothbrushes and annuals. At one point it was estimated that, if a fan had bought a piece of every type of merchandise on the market, she'd have spent over £1,000. Assuming the boys would only have a short shelf life, it made sense to capitalise while they were popular – something the Spice Girls were to do a couple of years later – and so, as the cash tills rang to the sound of Take That's music, the boys featured on everything, and everyone was laughing all the way to the bank.

Except that some were laughing a bit louder than others. Take That was still very much seen as Gary's vehicle and, as the songwriter for the group, he was earning a lot more than everyone else because of his composing royalties. In later years, in the wake of the comeback, Gary accepted that this had caused tensions but, back then, he was seen as the undisputed star and he was planning to hold on to that position. Even if Robbie hadn't precipitated matters by disappearing, tensions were building up that would eventually have flared up.

The girlfriend ban was publicly rescinded. Jason got together with a television presenter called Jenny Powell, although it didn't last very long. Gary was a little embarrassed when topless pictures appeared of an old girlfriend – Nicola Ladanowski – from the pre-Take That days, although it was pretty harmless stuff. Gary was now being spoken of as a real mover and shaker in the music industry, with insiders convinced that he would be the next George Michael. George had been the musical brains behind Wham! And, when that group broke up, he went on to massive things. For Gary, it was to turn out a little differently, although it all came right in the end.

Everything Changes got to UK0020No 1 and stayed in the charts for a phenomenal 78 weeks and, not surprisingly, cleaned up at the *Smash Hits* awards. Meanwhile, 'Relight My Fire', with Lulu on guest vocals, provided the Scottish singer with her first UK No 1 and everyone else with an intriguing rumour. Although Jason is often seen as the quietest member of the band and to date has not settled down, he was said to have had a fling with Lulu, something both remained remarkably coy about.

'He was half my age but he walked up to me, said I was sexy and that he fancied me rotten,' Lulu said in an interview some years later. 'He had a way of looking at me that woke something in me. It was electric. When I'm seventy, I'll look back and say, "Why the hell didn't I sleep with him?"' According to Howard, she did – or perhaps Howard was joking, too.

The year 1994 would be Take That's last as a five-piece in the first phase of their career but, outwardly, there was no indication that anything might be going wrong. They kicked off the year by performing a Beatles medley at the Brits in February, and it was pretty much one triumph after another after that. The boys were still touring almost constantly, appearing on more magazine covers, filming the 'Everything Changes' video and appearing all across Europe for the first time. Howard suffered his first dance injury when he did a flip and broke a finger. Gary won an Ivor Novello award for Songwriter of the Year and another for 'Pray'. There were appearances as far away as Japan and Australia, as well as plans to break America.

Take That were going from strength to strength. By the summer they were recording a new album. In October, their latest single, 'Sure', went to UK No 1 and stayed in the charts for a total of 15 weeks. They finished a phenomenal year by playing the Concert of Hope in front of Princess Diana, truly sensations and sensational. They had become Britain's most successful boy band ever. What could possibly go wrong?

CHAPTER EIGHT

EVERYTHING CHANGES

At the beginning of 1995 there was no sign that the most successful boy band to perform on the British stage was shortly to implode. Far from it. Take That were loved as few bands had been before, and they had yet to score their biggest success.

In 1995, Take That's third album, *Nobody Else*, appeared, with possibly their most striking cover to date – a pastiche of The Beatles' *Sgt Peppers Lonely Hearts Club Band*. The first single from the album, 'Sure', came out and leaped straight to UK No 1. And then 'Back for Good' came out. It was an absolute sensation, getting to No 1 in 31 countries and providing Take That with their only hit in the US, where it made the Top Ten. It was all the more ironic as they were actually about to implode.

'Back for Good' (written by Gary) was first performed in February 1995 at the Brit Awards. The crowd went wild, so much so that the single's release was brought forward to March. It sold 350,000 copies in its first week alone, almost as many as the rest of the Top Ten put together. It went on to sell over a million, won Best British Single and went on to feature in various television programmes, including *Explode Coracao* in Brazil, *Spaced* and *The Office*.

It was also covered by 89 different artists, including Boyz II Men and Robbie, who was to record a live version of it as the b-side of 'Angels'. Much later, Gary was to perform it with Coldplay in 2009. The video that accompanied it was also seen as a minor classic: shot in black and white, it had the boys running through the rain. It was a quite astonishing success but it also was also to mark the end of the first incarnation of the most successful boy band ever. Take That were about to split and it would be the best part of a decade and a half before four of them regrouped.

The problems with Robbie had been growing for some time. The band might not have known how out of control his drug-taking was becoming and they were choosing not to see how much he was drinking, but matters could not go on like this. Everyone knew it and, with that confrontation after his appearance at Glastonbury, that was it. Robbie was out.

'I had a night with Rob,' Mark recalled later on. 'We were in London and I remember staying up all night, talking and eating tuna sandwiches. It was the first time that he'd ever really said he was unhappy. The band was very regimented. When we were rehearsing for a tour, it felt like being in boot camp. And as we got older, Rob started to notice things in the world that he found more interesting than being in the band. About six months after that night, he left.'

It was not immediately apparent that this heralded the end, for now at least, of Take That. For a start, they had originally been conceived as a four-piece outfit and Robbie was the latecomer, so initially they kept going as a four-piece. They went on their 'Nobody Else' tour as Robbie licked his wounds and contemplated a future that was going to be very different. It seemed as if Take That might just pull it off.

But they didn't. There were too many stresses and strains: too much resentment had built up and the magic had gone. 'I'm reticent about speaking negatively about Take That,' said Jason a couple of years later, though he had clearly been feeling the strain, too. 'Nothing makes me cringe more than reading a sob story from a pop star about how awful it all was. But there were so many things wrong about it. I think Robbie was very accurate with what he said. Take That was led by a hierarchy: there was lots of bullying going on. Robbie saw through the bollocks that comes with being in a band of our type, the hypocrisy and artifice of it all.

'He wanted to be more real and it's difficult to be anything but plastic in a manufactured boy band. I don't want to say clichés. When Take That wasn't being ruled with an iron fist, when we weren't being divided in order that we could be conquered and therefore controlled, we were a real unit and I felt a genuine friendship. But being top of the charts, winning awards, that was always for other people. I didn't take gratification from it. I really didn't. I don't mean that in a modest way. For some reason, I just didn't feel it. I didn't feel involved, creatively or otherwise. I wasn't writing the songs. I was barely singing on them. I was the dancer. I went along with everything. I gave my power away and that's the worst thing you can do.'

Mark was unhappy, too. 'Jason and Howard were definitely better movers than me,' he said. 'Gary was a better singer. Robbie was a better singer. I didn't feel like I was... I think I added something to the band... I don't know... I don't know what my role was... I was very, very fortunate, to be honest. I don't think anybody ever felt we could actually lean on each other if there was a problem. If someone had a run-in with Nigel, we didn't back up our band member. We just all went a bit quiet. We didn't really know each other. We were more like workmates than friends. We thought we were friends, but we weren't really.'

Even Howard, who'd had a happier experience than Robbie or Jason, and who found it more difficult to deal with the break-up, came to realise that matters had not gone as they should. 'I think I have more positive memories than the others,' he said. 'I think, at the time, a lot of things went over my head. It's only with hindsight I was able to see how many things in the band were wrong. I don't think we looked after each other. We thought we did, and we thought we knew each other, but really we didn't know each other's inner feelings.'

Matters finally came to a head in February 1996, when a press conference was called in Manchester for the 13th (which also happened to be Robbie's 22nd birthday). There had been growing speculation in the press that the band was on the verge of a split and, although at first it had been officially denied, it was impossible to paper over the cracks any more. A statement went out: 'Unfortunately the rumours are true. "How Deep Is Your Love" is going to be our last single together and the *Greatest Hits* is going to be the last album, and from today... there's no more.'

It was Mark who confirmed the bad news and, oddly enough, Mark who dominated the press conference. With his easy charm, it was possible that the others felt he was best placed to put the news out in public. 'Well, first of all, we do care very much about our fans and we basically just decided – there's been a number of factors that have made us change,' he said. 'Also, we're all gonna stay around. It's not the end and we want the fans to know that we all have plans to do other things but a number of factors have brought us to this decision. We've decided the time is right. We've done all that we can do as Take That. We took it to a level well beyond any of our expectations and, I suppose, beyond many of your expectations. There have been a number of other factors, which we don't really want to go into, but I'm sure you know what's going on behind the scenes but, basically we just want to reassure the fans that it isn't the end. For now, it is the end of Take That but we'll all still be around – our mugs will turn up on TVs and doing things for numbers of years to come. We're not totally ruling out Take That just for now – we've taken it as far as we can go at the moment but there may be more to come.'

Although it was to be years before the full story and all the backstage tensions came out, in hindsight what was really going through everyone's mind was plain to see. Howard was taking it especially badly, and he said as much. 'I think, like Gary said, we've all got individual feelings. I mean, I'm sure we are a little bit upset, especially me,' he began. 'While I'm very emotional at the moment, I know that it's the best time now to finish at the top. We've always said that we would finish on top and it's very good for our careers ahead of us so I think we're making the right move.'

What about the fans? There had been massive upset when Robbie had left just over six months earlier: would provision be made for them? 'I'll say that we hope the fans will understand that we feel we have done all we can do as Take That,' said Mark. 'We do very much care for the welfare of our fans and, if there are any problems, I'm sure we can set up phone lines or whatever may be needed to sort that out, definitely.' In fact, that wasn't to be the half of it. A wave of near-hysteria swept some portions of the population when the news broke.

There were, too, various loaded questions. Who, they were asked, was going to have the most successful solo career? At the time, it seemed self-evident. 'Like Mark says, this is a decision that we've all come to and we've not had much time to think about it,' said Gary. 'But as usual, I've got loads of material and I hope to have a single out by the summer, followed very closely by the album, and I'll hopefully do some concerts this year.' All this was, indeed, to happen, but Gary was going to find it a lot colder out there on his own than he could have imagined.

The others were prepared to have a go as well, of course. 'That would be a plan for us. I know that's something I'd like to do, definitely,' said Mark. 'I'm very inexperienced so I'm not rushing into it. I've not had the experience of Gaz but luckily I've watched him over the last five years and pinched a few chords off him and a few of his songs, too, that he doesn't know about. I've got the melodies in me head.'

He accepted, though, that they might all, as the questioner put it, disappear without trace. 'There is every chance of that,' he said. 'With Gary, he's managed to build up so much material and he is such a good songwriter. But for us there is every chance we may disappear but we don't want that to be the case. We want to have a go at doing it ourselves now and it's not just a decision that Gary's made. It's a decision that came from us all. We just felt, as I said, that as Take That we did all we could but as individuals we could do a lot more.'

Jason had something to say as well. 'You know, we're all quite naturally going to have apprehensions about it but we're trying to look at it all positively and I think it's important for us all to state that here,' he said. 'We don't want any negativity. It was a very positive thing when we set out. We've achieved all that we set out to achieve – well, more – and not it's brilliant because it's like we've got a new lifestyle, where we feature as individuals. We're trying to look at it positively...

'We took Take That as far as we wished to take it and so, when we say it's the end, it may be the end of Take That for now, but there is every chance at the end of the day of doing one of those comeback things, or there's every chance of us all pursuing solo careers. When we say it's the end, it's just the end of Take That.

'Can I just say, sorry to keep stressing it, but this is

a really positive thing for us. It's definitely a step on. We know there [are] so many sob stories with has-been pop stars – you know, complaining about loss of money through fast cars, fast women and fast living. We would like to say today that we've had a brilliant time and we've got no sob stories, and that's really wicked. A few of us have got fast cars but we're still waiting for the fast women. It's just a really positive vibe and we're all looking forward to going and finding it in other ways.'

There it was. Jason, in some ways the most publicity-shy of the boys, had already mentioned the possibility of a comeback, and it was something Gary latched on to, too. 'Like Mark said, it's something that's been growing over the last six months but, you know, it is a career move for all of us,' he said. 'You know, our dream is that, after five or ten years, we'll come back and do it all again.'

That, of course, was exactly what happened, but that was a good decade off. In the wilderness years that were to follow, the boys must have thought they were being insanely optimistic. For now, it was a question of winding everything up. They released their *Greatest Hits* compilation with a new recording, a cover of the Bee Gees' 'How Deep Is Your Love?' (their final UK No 1 in their first incarnation) and gave a last performance in April 1996 in Amsterdam. And that was that. Take That was no more.

To say that their fans were distraught does not begin to sum it up. The Samaritans were so overwhelmed with calls that they had to set up a special helpline. It is not putting it too strongly to say that shock reverberated throughout the teen community. Some remember it well to this day.

'People say they remember where they were when JFK and John Lennon were shot, and I will always remember where I was when Take That broke up,' said Michelle Latham, who went on to become a childminder in Worksop, Notts. 'I watched the press conference live on MTV and didn't stop crying for two weeks.'

'I was so distraught when Take That broke up that the head teacher of my primary school organised an assembly to tell the school to be nice to me,' said Selina Maycock, from Rotherham in South Yorkshire. 'When I first found out about the split, I cried into my Take That duvet on my bunk-bed for hours.'

They were not alone. But at that point, no one knew of the tensions behind the scenes that had simply become too much for the boys to cope with.

On top of that, boy bands do have a short shelf life: no one had expected them to go on for ever. They'd experienced success beyond their wildest dreams: in total they had sold more than 25 million records since they had formed 5 years ago and, if they were sensible, none of them would ever have to work again. That's not to say they didn't want to, however. All of them were very keen, indeed, to make their mark, in whichever form they chose to do it. It was just that it was going to take them an awful lot longer than they'd thought.

CHAPTER NINE

THE WILDERNESS YEARS

And so Take That was no more. Robbie's star was shortly to rise very swiftly, but the four other boys were not to fare so well, all but fading to obscurity until they were catapulted back to fresh heights of fame.

The person expected to become a solo star was Gary. He was certainly the most gifted songwriter and all-round musician among them. His problem, however, was that he didn't have Robbie's charisma. That was what propelled his former bandmate to greatness – that and the song 'Angels', which was not only one of the best pop songs of the decade, but was extremely timely in appearing just at the time of Princess Diana's death. Without wishing to be cruel, Robbie was lucky in his timing. Gary was not.

As mentioned earlier, Gary's first two singles, 'Forever Love' and 'Love Won't Wait' (written by Madonna and recorded by her, too, although never released) both got to UK No 1, as did his first album, *Open Road*. He did well, too, with another couple of singles, 'So Help Me Girl' and the album's title song, and with his second album, *Twelve Months, Eleven Days*. But there were intense pressures, which sometimes got Gary down.

'When the band split up, everyone was looking at me to be the next George Michael, the next Elton John,' he said. 'It was like pulling a rabbit out of a hat. It was a horrible period and I was under incredible pressure. I realised I had to have a year off for my sanity. I am very driven and need success. I may seem laid back but I'm extremely competitive. I've a lot of confidence and self-belief. I'm desperate for success and I'm really going for it.' But fate had other plans.

Gary began to settle down personally, too. In 1999, he married Dawn Andrews, who he'd become close to on the 'Nobody Else' tour in 1995, when she was a backing dancer. Howard was best man and DJ. 'We met when I was seventeen, during a video shoot, and I thought she was beautiful,' Gary recalled just after they got engaged. 'Then a few years later, we bumped into each other again. It went on like that for years. We kept catching each other's eye. On the last tour, we ordered fifteen dancers and let Jason Orange audition them. We were putting our orders in: "Get me a dark one, get me a blonde one," or whatever. Jason said he'd sorted us all out but when I turned up, I saw Dawn. She wasn't the one he'd ordered for me but we just got to know each other. That's when we became inseparable. I've been pestering her to get married for four years. I know she's the one for me. She's absolutely perfect. She understands me and that's why I want her to be my wife. I came clean about my past with her and told her I'd been a really naughty boy.' (Gary was referring to the fact that he'd dabbled in drugs.)

The proposal was an unusual one. 'I asked her to marry me after we'd ordered a Chinese at home,' said Gary. 'We were waiting for it to be delivered and I said, "I've got an idea – let's get married." We went to Tiffany's in New York and got a ring for about £10,000. We are planning to get married at my house in Cheshire with the reception there and the wedding on the front lawn. I really want children very soon. I'd never have dreamed of saying that a year ago. The biggest thing I love about Dawn is that she's still working as a dancer. It can be a shit job but she's her own person. I am very aware that some people would want to be with me because of my fame or my money but she's not like that.'

In fact, Gary was feeling very nostalgic about the years in Take That. 'We were so young and naïve then,' he recalled. 'We were all single and it was every guy's dream. We loved every minute of it: we had money and girls all over the place. I do miss the madness but it all seems a blur now. It's like it wasn't me. What I miss is the camaraderie of five best friends all in it together. When you get to No 1 as a solo artist, you just kind of go, "Hoorah!" But when you're in a band, it's different. You all go mad and hug each other and go out and celebrate. It's a team effort – you feel like you've achieved it together. It is quite lonely being a solo artist. With Jason, Robbie, Mark and Howard, we were all in the same boat and having the same experiences. I think I would have freaked out if I had gone through that on my own. Mentally, it's been hard to adjust. For me, the best moments were not when we won Brit Awards, but when we were all alone together in hotel rooms, having fun. We were like five brothers – we'd stick up for one another and that was a wonderful experience.'

Robbie heads to the high court in London in 1997.   © *Rex Features*

Bare faced cheek. Robbie pulls one of his famous moons. This one is for the opposition after scoring a goal for his favourite team Port Vale in a testimonial game.

© *Rex Features*

Top: Robbie adds to the many tattoos adorning his body.

Bottom: Gary Barlow and Robbie Williams reunited at the Concert of Hope charity concert in 1997 with Denise Van Outen.

Top: Robbie takes a bath on The Big Breakfast. © *Alpha Press*

Bottom: Howard Donald DJs in Germany in 2002. © *Rex Features*

Top: Over three nights in August 2003, Robbie performed live to over 375,000 people at Knebworth, staging the UK's biggest-ever pop concert to date.

© *Rex Features*

Bottom Left: With his song-writing partner, Guy Chambers, before their dramatic split.

Bottom Right: Robbie shops with Elton John, one of his richest fans.

Top: The new Take That take the train to promote their comeback album.

© *Rex Features*

Bottom: Smart-dressed men. A newly-confident Take That.   © *Rex Features*

Top: Take That back in concert in London.   © *PA Photos*

Bottom: The album was launched in France in late 2008.   © *Rex Features*

Top: Taking a break outside the recording studio in 2008. © *Rex Features*

Bottom: Gary, Jason and Robbie filming the new video for the new Take That. © *Rex Features*

Given that he was speaking just a couple of years after Take That's break-up, it is perhaps no surprise that the group reformed. At that stage, Gary seemed to be on the verge of solo success, but he was clearly missing his bandmates. It just wasn't the same without them.

Gary was in danger of sounding a little patronising, too. His former bandmates were finding life hard after the break-up and, although Gary, too, was to suffer, at that stage it didn't seem to be the case. 'It's so difficult to remember that we had the world in our hands and that makes me sad,' he said. 'I feel sorry for Mark and Howard and I really want to help them but I know that would be a backwards step. When Robbie left, we became four but it was like having one of your legs cut off. We could tell we were losing him – he wanted more than the Take That lifestyle. What I remember most is that the lads used to think I was mean with my money. It's true that I had a mobile phone when I joined the group but I was on the dole. So when they used my phone, I admit I used to charge them to make calls. But that was years ago and now I think I'm a pretty extravagant person.'

Indeed, Gary had by now amassed a £20 million fortune. But he wanted continuing career success and, although he was to achieve it behind the scenes, things did not go according to plan.

In 2000, Gary and Dawn had their first child, Daniel. Two years later, Emily came along and, in 2009, they had their third child, Daisy. Over the next few years, when his work life was not going quite as well as it had done, his family were to prove a great comfort to him. Indeed, some years later, before he met Ayda, Robbie was to say that he would swap all his success for the happiness Gary had found in his personal life.

But now things were beginning to go wrong. The open warfare with Robbie was beginning and Robbie was beginning to win. Totally unexpectedly, a backlash began to develop against Gary, with the result that he quit as a singer – not that he had much choice. BMG/RCA terminated his contract, while Gary received no support at all from anyone, getting little radio play for his work.

'I talked to promoters about doing a small-scale tour,' Gary said many years later. 'I explored every possible avenue, even shopping around songs for other people to record but, within a couple of months, it became clear that there was no way forward for me. When you're hot and are having hits, the industry can't get enough. When you're cold, it's like having some disease. No one wants any association with you at all. It's as if you've been fired for stealing out of the till. It's instant, brutal. You're unemployable. You don't even get the gold watch and the handshake. But that's not the point. My issue was that I wanted to work and couldn't. That was the most upsetting thing for me, music being all I know.'

Gary was deeply wounded by this, and no wonder. Having been hyped up as the talent of the band, to see the music industry all but wash its hands of him was extremely hurtful. He later revealed that, when it happened, he retreated to his Cheshire home, Delamere Manor, vowing never to go on stage again. He began comfort eating, gaining five stone, until some years later Dawn got him to a doctor and on to a fitness regime. He was to become as svelte as any of them but, for now, it was very hard to see that there was any future for him in music.

Gary also encountered a good deal of unpleasantness at that time – not least because Robbie was very publicly winning the war between the two of them. 'It's one thing getting dropped, but what it filters down to is walking along the street and having people shout, "How's Robbie?"' he said. 'Or you go in a shop and they put on his CD the moment they see you. That's what made me reclusive. There's a meanness in Britain. People relish your situation. You end up embarrassed to be who you are. It got to the point where I wouldn't even use my credit card over the phone, 'cause I was ashamed to say my name. It was an odd, depressing, very negative time.'

Home was a great comfort during this difficult time, as Gary was to tell the *Chester Chronicle*, as his life gradually began to improve. 'My regular pub has always been The Goshawk in Mouldsworth and I'm just never bothered in there,' he said. 'The only other place I'm never bothered is London, because it's so busy you can just mingle in. I love the fact that you can do all this and still have a relatively normal life here. I've probably expected a bit much of our local pubs over the years. I've had Charlotte Church in there, I took the whole of Blue once, I've had Westlife there and somehow they just always seem to come over and say, "I'll get you a quiet table in the corner."'

Gary also tried his hand at acting. In 2000, he appeared in the 150th episode of *Heartbeat*, playing the role of Micky Shannon alongside the TV veteran Bill Maynard (the lovable rogue Claude Jeremiah Greengrass), then 71.

'I was very apprehensive about appearing on telly,' Gary said in an interview at the time. 'Put me on stage at Wembley Arena and I'm fine, but acting is something I've never done before. That has never been where my talents lie. I mean, when I was in the nativity play at school, the teacher cast me as a sheep! I must admit I was reluctant to do it. When my nan was alive, I used to visit her on a Sunday night and watch *Heartbeat* with her. I didn't think I could act and had always vowed that I'd never try it. When I was discussing the possibility of making music shows with Granada last year, they suggested I should make a guest appearance in the show. What tempted me was that I could sing in it. I love the music in *Heartbeat* and that's another reason why I changed my mind.

'Learning my lines and getting the patter was hard enough, but the most difficult part was being a passenger in that car with Bill – his eyesight isn't what it used to be, bless him. At first, I assumed there would be stuntmen to do it... How wrong I was. We had to bomb down this road and I was clinging to my seatbelt. Bill and I hit it off straight away, though. We had this witty repartee going on, and working with him really helped me to relax and get into the role. I'd studied Sean Bean, because he's a northerner, and I'm a great fan of his. Not that I'm anti-southerner or anything – it was just nice to be working among my own for a while. The rest of the cast were fun to work with, too. They kept playing practical jokes on me, such as filling a bag I had to sling over my shoulder with rocks. When I had to be handcuffed at the end, they pretended they'd lost the key, so I was stuck there for an hour and a half in handcuffs. One of the best bits about making *Heartbeat* was my new hairstyle, though. I had to have my hair slicked back into a duck's ass, a quiff. It was wild.'

Gary was beginning to get things in perspective, too. 'In a way, the knocks and criticism I've received have been good for me,' he said. 'I used to think that being famous was about going on *Top of the Pops* every week. Now I know what it's all about. When you start out and release a single that doesn't chart, you think you've failed, but at least no one knows. When you're already known like me and take a wrong turning, everyone's there laughing. I won't let that put me off. I always dreamed of making a career as a pop star and I succeeded. Music will always be my life. I've learned a lot about fame. Even if I reached another level of success right now, it would be different to my Take That days. I used to appeal to a teenage audience but, on tour before Christmas, I noticed that the crowd was mainly twenty-year-olds. I don't care – I just want them to like my music.'

In 2001, Gary moved to Los Angeles with his family and began to work as a songwriter for other artists, among them Delta Goodrem, Elton John, Donny Osmond and Christina Aguilera. He also became president of the True North Music Company, a production and publishing business he'd set up with his friend Eliot Kennedy (who'd co-written and produced 'Everything Changes') and writer/musician Tim Daniel. It was all a perfectly respectable performance – but it wasn't exactly what had gone before.

Still, it did give him time to regroup and his relative anonymity was something of a boon. 'I didn't wear socks for eight months,' he said. 'The weather was always fine. I could walk around the supermarket unnoticed. We even made friends with the neighbours, who knew nothing of who I was and had no fixed opinion of me. I loved that. They were spending time with us just because we're nice people and they enjoyed our company, nothing more.'

But he did persevere with his music. Other artists he worked with included Blue, Atomic Kitten, Lara Fabian and Charlotte Church. Some of his songs were huge successes: 'Leave Right Now' by Will

Young, for example, and 'Lost Without You' by Delta Goodrem. There were rumours that he wrote a song for Eurovision in 2004 and he collaborated on the pop musical *Love Shack* in 2005.

But progress was slow. 'It didn't happen overnight by any means, but people were kind enough to start giving me bits and pieces [songwriting commissions, production work] here and there,' said Gary. 'And, of course, it was helped by the fact that, three or four years on, our records were still on the radio. It was like they thought, "Yeah, he used to write great stuff. I wonder what he's doing now?" and then picked up the phone to give me a call. I didn't sing a note in six years, not even on a demo. I locked the door on that side of me, told everyone around me I didn't want to do it any more. I even convinced myself that it was true.'

Although the bitterness between Gary and Robbie began to calm down, it was still there in the background for years. 'Oh yeah,' Gary said in one interview. 'Me and Robbie used to play terrible tricks on each other. I took Robbie's album back to a music shop once and... stupid, stupid things! Things you wouldn't dream of doing as a thirty-seven-year-old bloke. Quite seriously I'd do it, as well. It wouldn't be as a joke.'

Gary moved back to the UK and, although still living in Cheshire, took a very different turn when he began to contribute restaurant reviews to the west London magazine *Grove*. And there was some consolation to be found in the fact that, in 2003, a remix of 'Love Won't Wait' did very well in America. But he missed the group, he missed the glory days and he wanted to return to the melee. Eventually, the family moved from their home in Cheshire down to London – and one of the most popular groups Britain has ever produced rose to glory once more.

Mark had been the heartthrob of the group and, as such, had been expected to achieve some degree of solo success. As with the others, however, it eluded him, although he did well initially. Mark was actually the third member of the group, after Robbie and Gary, to release a solo single, 'Child', which got to UK No 3. His second single, 'Clementine', also got to UK No 3. But then he, too, began to experience problems. His debut album, *Green Man*, only made it to UK No 33, and, after his single 'I Am What I Am' struggled to UK No 29, Mark was dropped by BMG Records in late 1997. 'An absolute low point,' he said in 2008. 'Everything that had happened up until then had been positive. I didn't know there could be a downside. To find yourself making records on your own that sell three copies... It hurts. But you've got to hit the bottom before you can rebuild.'

Although a veil is drawn over it these days, Mark dropped out of sight for the next few years, basing himself at his beautiful home in the Lake District and wondering what to do next. The answer came in 2002, when he was invited to appear on *Celebrity Big Brother*. He did it and won with 77 per cent of the vote, beating the television presenter Les Dennis, who himself was having a very public meltdown over the break-up of his relationship with the actress Amanda Holden. Mark was so moved by the public vote that he burst into tears afterwards, saying that he didn't think he had any fans left after the break-up of Take That. 'I've been quiet for four years,' he said when he came out of the house. 'If I had not gone in the house, I would have been at home trying to make another album.'

Mark's win illustrated two points. The first was that Mark (and by extension, the rest of the boys) still occupied a very definite place in the nation's affections, so perhaps no one should have been surprised when their reunion went so spectacularly well a couple of years down the line. Secondly, it was another step on the road to reconciling with Robbie. Mark and Robbie had had a strong bond when they were in Take That and Mark had been more upset than anyone by Robbie's departure. Gradually, the two started to be close once more.

Mark appeared on stage with Robbie at Knebworth and, on the back of this, started the second stint of his solo career. He was signed by Island/Universal Records and released a single, 'Four Minute Warning', which got to UK No 5. A second solo album, *In Your Own Time*, came out in November 2003, but it only got to UK No 59, and a second solo single, 'Alone Without You', only made it to UK No 26. For a second time Mark found himself dropped by his record label, but this time he started his own label, Sedna Records. 'Doing it properly isn't cheap,' he said. 'These are my indulgences. I don't have a Ferrari, I have two albums.' In fact, he went on to record a third album, the aptly named *How the Mighty Fall*, which was recorded at Sunset Studios in Los Angeles. He is still taking his music seriously: whatever happens with Take That, there are still plans for a solo career.

The travails in Mark's personal life were recounted earlier in this book and it is to be hoped that his marriage will survive. However, in the wake of the break-up of Take That, he had two other serious relationships: first with an art student called Joanna Kelly, and then with the actress, Chloe Bailey. He was with Joanna for eight years and friends thought they would marry but, in 2000, she decided their relationship wasn't going anywhere and left.

Mark's friends were shocked. 'Everyone thought that they were inseparable,' said one. 'Mark thought the world of Joanna. She was his rock, very sensible and together, the perfect loyal girlfriend. She met him at the height of Take That in about 1994 and, when Robbie left the following year and the band started to go downhill, she really became the strength behind him.' Joanna returned to her home town of Bury in Lancashire, where she started to run a company called Earth Mother with her sister Rachel.

Mark met Chloe the same year, when she was working in London's fashionable Met Bar. The pair clicked straight away. Mark was going through something of a reclusive stage at the time, having grown a beard and shunning the limelight but, for a while, the pair were happy.

'He wasn't hugely famous then, just a wonderful, sweet bloke,' Chloe said in an interview after the split. 'I didn't have a clue who he was at first – he had long hair and a beard. But I fell in love with

Mark within days of meeting him. I have never been more in love in my life and said "yes" [to moving in with him].'

It was a very passionate relationship. 'We were madly in love,' said Chloe. 'We didn't need anybody else. We could talk about anything. He is a really spiritual person who believes in karma and Buddhism. We would lock ourselves away in bed for the whole day doing what normal couples in love do. We couldn't keep our hands off each other. There were days when we never got out of bed. We would make love endlessly, up to six times. He was a fantastic lover. He had a wonderful body. He may seem the smallest of the guys from Take That but he was very muscly and athletic. The only exercise he ever did then was have sex with me and we did it so often, it kept him in perfect shape. We were so in love, we didn't want anybody else. It was pure bliss.'

Mark was living in some style in his Lake District home but it was telling that, at that stage, he seemed almost to want to block out the past. 'The manor had chandeliers, rustic tiled floors and an Aga – but nothing to hint at where the cash to buy it had come from. There was no sign of Take That at all. No discs on the wall or anything,' said Chloe. 'And Mark rarely saw or spoke of his old bandmates. He would play charity football with Jason Orange. But they never came around to the house. He didn't act like a star. Mark's only really annoying point was his obsession with cleaning. He was great around the house and would do the cooking but, as soon as you'd eaten a meal, he would whisk your plate away and clean it. He did all the cleaning. He'd have it done before I even had chance to offer. He had this real paranoia about germs.'

But at that point at least, they were really happy. 'We hardly left the house,' said Chloe. 'Sometimes I would go to London for castings or he would speak to record companies about securing a deal, but all we needed was each other. We would go shopping, potter around markets or go to antique shops. We were blissfully happy.'

What brought it all to an end was *Celebrity Big Brother*. The fact that Mark had so little to remind him of his time with Take That strongly implied that he'd been extremely distressed when his time with the band came to an end, and that he couldn't bear to think about it. In the wake of *Celebrity Big Brother*, however, he tasted fame again – and found he liked it. A new career beckoned: it seemed that success was not just a thing of the past after all. Because he and Chloe had been living such a secluded life together, when real life intruded, it ended up tearing them apart.

'The bubble burst,' said Chloe sadly. 'He enjoyed being famous. For the first time, he started wanting to go to film premieres. He'd said in the house that he liked *Lord of the Rings* so they sent tickets to the premiere. He even bought me a vintage dress to wear. I loved the dress but realised his work was taking over. His focus had changed and then I got a play to do in London. For the first time, we started to argue. It was a horrible, sad time.'

And so the relationship came to an end. 'I was devastated,' said Chloe. 'I will never forget going back to the house to collect my stuff. I remember driving away and seeing him crying on the doorstep. Mark had put fame before me. It was hard to watch him on TV or listen to his music – I was too distraught. He chose fame over me. He dumped me and wrecked my life. We had planned to spend the rest of our days together. We would have got married. Suddenly, it was over. He ended it.'

And so another chapter in Mark's life came to a close. But like Gary, he found he'd been missing the limelight much more than he'd realised. He, too, was ready to return to the stage once more.

Howard Donald and Jason Orange were both to do

wildly different things in their ten years off. Initially, Howard was very badly affected by the split: so much so that he later confessed to having considered suicide. 'I didn't want us to split ... I was pissed off,' he said. 'I walked out the hotel and I wanted to throw myself into the Thames ... but I thought, "Knowing me, I'll end up in the middle of the river and the tide will go out and I'll be in the papers stuck in the Thames mud looking like a cock."'

Mercifully, nothing so drastic ensued but he was forced to find a very different way to earn his daily bread. It certainly hit him hard: 'People around you think it'll never end,' he said years later. 'And when it does, they want to know, "What are you going to do now? What's your plan?" I didn't have one, which made me feel I'd failed.'

In the immediate aftermath of the split, Howard recorded a single, 'Speak Without Words', that still has not been released to this day. He also recorded a solo album and video for the single, which he funded himself and which also remain unreleased. Eventually, he decided to take another route all together and began to work as a DJ under the title DJ HD, something he had actually done before joining Take That. He became the resident DJ at Nigel Martin-Smith's nightclub Essential, in Manchester. It was a success and Howard began to build up a large fan base in this new role, especially in Germany, and it's something he continues to do to this day when not appearing with Take That.

'I've been DJing since the late 1980s, playing at any party I could get an audience to listen, so it's not something new that I have taken up,' he said in an interview in 2009. 'I also used to play at some of the band aftershow parties in the 1990s and then, when we broke up, I obviously decided to take things a bit more seriously, mainly because I have always loved DJing. It's a totally different scenario [from being in Take That] and very difficult to compare, because performing on stage is very rehearsed and a much bigger audience, so you don't have the same interaction with your crowd as when you DJ.

'I also find that, as a DJ, you have to roll with things and potentially change what you are doing if it's not working, so it's very difficult to predict. It difficult to say who has influenced me because I have always had my own idea of the kind of music I want to make and play, but I have a lot of people I've listened to over the years which I am a fan of, including Kraftwerk, Jean Michel Jarre and Phoenix, who are a French electronic guitar group, then more recently AIR, another French electronic band, and Muse.' Later, he brought his two skills together and started to produce other people's music as well.

Like the others, Howard went through a series of serious relationships although, unlike them, he has yet to settle down. The first affair was with Victoria Piddington, who was a Take That fan, with whom he had a daughter, Grace, born in 1999. The pair lived together for a while but ultimately split. Howard then acquired a German girlfriend, Marie Christine Musswessels, who was a student. She, too, bore him a daughter, Lola, in 2005, although they, too, were to split, in 2009.

His former dance partner Jason Orange also took a very different route in the wake of the band's split. The only one who did not pursue a solo career in music, he decided to travel the world instead and become an actor. First, he went backpacking around the Far East, something that would have been inconceivable when he was still with the boys. 'Travelling opens your eyes – you see new things all the time and you learn,' he said.

Then, with the actor Max Beesley, who had played percussion for Take That, he went to New York, where they both studied acting, which resulted in Jason landing roles first in the play *Let's All Go to the*

Fair at London's Royal Court theatre and then as the bad-boy DJ Brent Moyer in a TV version of Lynda La Plante's thriller *Killer Net*, both in 1998. He also played a mouthy street poet in Jim Kenworth's *Gob* at the King's Head theatre in London.

Jason kept a diary of the run-up to the premiere of *Gob*, which actually turned out to be a great success, even though it was very different from the glory days. 'At last! We're in the King's Head theatre, it's chaos, the set is still under construction and everyone is running around,' he wrote. 'Tom Hayes, my co-star, and I try to get used to the confined space. The stage is tiny. It's rather bizarre after playing 20,000-seater stadiums to be on a stage where the audience are perilously close to the stage – they will be able to see the terror in my eyes. We try a run-through, it feels good but we are desperate to get before an audience. We retreat, exhausted, to Pizza Express, with James, our director, and Jim, the writer.'

He carried on the next day. 'Up at nine, I have a cup of herbal tea and a banana for strength. I have a press photo-call at lunchtime. Tom and I are met by a wall of telephoto lenses. Tom looks shocked, but it's nothing I haven't seen before. We clown around, mugging faces and doing handstands, the lights flash and shouts of "Over here, Jason," and "Do it again for me!" remind me of the heady days of Take That. I know they'll use the picture of me pulling a totally ridiculous face! It's the first performance tonight. Just before it starts, I'm very nervous. It's packed and really loud. Suddenly, I feel strangely calm. I finish the show exhausted but on a real high. Michael, the producer, cracks open the Bollinger and we let our hair down.'

Although he was to maintain a very low profile in the years leading up to the reunion, Jason, too, revealed that it was not impossible that one day Take That would reform. 'We spent so long together that we needed our own space when we broke up,' he said in 1999. 'There was no major fallout or showdown... We're all doing our own thing. If there was any real friendship there, we can always resume it in five years' time.'

After that, however, Jason seemed happy to steer clear of the limelight. He went to South Trafford College, where he studied psychology and sociology. Indeed, in many ways, he found anonymity a relief. 'When I first joined the band, I was mad for it,' he said. 'I kept a scrapbook of all our magazine front covers. I bought into the idea wholesale. But ten years on, I found I loved being a private person again. I loved walking through town unrecognised, unmolested. To be honest, I think fame is shit. I wouldn't recommend it to anyone. I know it's a huge aspiration for a lot of young people these days, but really I can't think of one redeeming feature it has other than that of a quick ego caress or being able to jump the queue at a club. Otherwise, it sucks.'

Unlike the other members of the band, Jason has never settled down. In Take That's first incarnation, he ran a bit wild, having a fling with, among others, Lulu, but age seems to have mellowed him. 'Jason used to be the stud of the group but he's totally changed,' said Howard. 'Maybe it's getting older or maybe it's because he's given up the booze. He's given up the ladies – and he's single. The drive from the old days seems to have died down.'

'When we're on tour now, he's in his hotel room with the "Do Not Disturb" sign out,' said Mark. 'We think he's making pots of tea for himself in there. He was the wild one. But when we tackle him, he's like, "I was just reading and went to bed early."'

Jason never quite settled into another role outside Take That in the way that Howard did. But he didn't need to. For a near-miracle was about to take place.

CHAPTER TEN

FOR THE RECORD

It all started, funnily enough, with a documentary. The year was 2005 and it had been a full decade since Robbie had walked out of the band, leading, ultimately, to its break up. Take That was just a pleasant cultural memory. The fans had long since grown up and moved on; the band members had their various projects and Robbie was doing his thing in Los Angeles. The events of the past were just that – in the past.

Even so, an independent production company called Back2back Productions thought there might still be some mileage in Take That. The only member to have achieved significant solo success on stage was Robbie, although Gary was doing well behind the scenes and there was a certain degree of curiosity from the public about what they'd all been up to. And so, on 17 November 2005, more than six million viewers tuned in to see what the boys had been getting up to. It would have consequences that none of those taking part could possibly have foreseen.

All five members of Take That took part, along with their erstwhile manager, although Robbie was filmed separately from the rest. Each one described how he had been discovered by Nigel Martin-Smith, while Martin-Smith revealed that it was after he'd received Gary's demo tape containing 'A Million Love Songs' that he'd realised he had a potential success on his hands. They talked about their early years in gay clubs and their first single, the less than earth-shattering 'Do What U Like'. They talked about memories of teen hysteria, of Lulu, of Robbie's departure and subsequent drug abuse.

The documentary-makers had managed to track down a huge amount of old footage, which they interspersed with the members of Take That recalling what they had all been doing when they first got together. This footage consisted not only of the boys in their glory days, but much older film – Gary winning musical competitions and Jason in a very early television appearance. The boys all spoke frankly about what had happened to them, about their hopes and regrets, and about what it had all meant.

They started with the earliest days. 'By the time I was driving, seventeen, I had my own act, which was singing cover versions, you know – "The Wind Beneath My Wings", whatever,' Gary recalled. '*Pop Idol* stuff. And that was kind of my living.' The programme then cut to a talent show, with Philip Schofield saying, 'So, next a senior entry written by fifteen-year-old Gary Barlow,' followed by footage of the young prodigy.

Jason was next. 'I was dancing in and around clubs in Manchester,' he said. 'I started dancing when I was, like, thirteen – breakdancing and bodypopping and stuff, and I started dancing on TV shows.' There was footage of that, too, with Jason saying, 'Hello, my name is Jason. Jason Orange. I come from Manchester. I decorate in the daytime and I dance at night time.'

Then it was Mark's turn. 'I worked in a bank at that time,' he said. 'It was a way to break out of that mould, you know. And I just thought, "Oh yeah!" You know? "Why not?"'

'I was a vehicle painter, mending cars for a living,' said Howard. 'And at the same time, I was dancing but obviously not professional. Luckily for me, he [his boss] gave me half a day off. If he hadn't given me half a day off, I would've been looking at someone else. I would have been looking at a boy group on TV saying, "Oh yeah, he's gay, he's gay."'

And finally, it was Robbie. 'I seem to think that my mum heard about it on a radio station one morning and sent my CV off,' he said. 'Which, of course, was extensive – my work at the rep. And... "Have you seen my Dodger? I was fantastic!" And she sent the CV off, and then I got a call, I believe, from Nigel Martin-Smith to go up and be interviewed.'

'A friend of mine brought me a clip out of a newspaper,' said Jason. 'And it was Nigel's advertisement for this band.'

'I can remember feeling incredibly intimidated and nervous about going into this guy's office,' Robbie added. 'And then he didn't do anything to put that at ease in any way.'

'I suppose my first meeting with Nigel was one of those milestones in life, really,' said Gary (accurately).

And then Nigel Martin-Smith came on. 'Gary was basically doing the clubs, working the proper working-men's clubs,' he said. 'And he came in to see me about doing bit parts 'cause he'd got an Equity [actors union] card. He mentioned right at the very end that, "Oh, by the way, I write music." And so I said, "Oh, right, nice one. Have you got any tapes or anything?" So he left me a tape.'

Back to Gary: 'And he took this tape off me like he'd been given a thousand of these things,' he said. 'He just kind of tossed it onto one side of his desk.'

'This track came on,' said Nigel, 'and I thought, "That's not him. That's not this kid I've just seen."'

'I had a show that night so I was washing me Ford Orion,' said Gary. 'I could hear the phone ringing.'

Cut to Nigel: 'Just about that tape that you gave me – what's on it?'

'I said, "It's me,"' said Gary.

Nigel: 'So I said, "That 'Million Love Songs' track – is that you singing?" He went, "Yeah."'

Gary: '"But who's made all the music behind it?" I said, "I do it all in my bedroom. It's just me, the whole thing."'

Nigel: 'So I said, "Can you come in straight – can you come back?"'

Gary: 'I said, "Absolutely. What time?" "Ten o'clock, please, come back and see me."'

Nigel: 'And the demo for "Million Love Songs" – he had a little studio at home – was exactly the same as what went on to be the hit record.'

Robbie and Gary shared their earliest memories of each other, too. 'There was this guy with, I've gotta say, a Morrissey haircut,' said Robbie. 'And I was thinking, "Twat." And now I'm not, you know? It's like, I try to have it cut the same today. And it was Gary and he'd got blond hair, I seem to remember. And he'd got these Converse hundreds on with an Italia ninety jumper, if I seem to remember correctly. And I just looked at his trainers and I thought, "Knob."'

Gary was a little more polite. 'Robbie had all the mod, the cool gear on. And Jason, real natural physique,' he said. 'And Howard just looked like a model. They looked like they all looked after themselves. They dressed well; they were all quite fit. And that was the first time I was kind of, "God, I've gotta work at this."'

Nigel, of course, was the one with the clearest idea of what they were all getting in to. He summed it up succinctly, too. 'I can remember now very clearly saying to them, "You know, in five years time, if it is a success, you'll probably hate each other. You'll definitely hate me, because that's what happens. But we'll all be very wealthy."' In fact, it was really only Robbie who hated him and even that was cooling down now.

Right from the start, it was hard work. 'We had this choreographer who was a nice guy, but Nigel had ordered him to make us do press-ups every morning as soon as we got in there,' said Howard.

Gary agreed. 'This guy had us doing press-ups, sit-ups, routines till seven in the evening. Oh, it was horrible.'

Strangely enough, it was Robbie who had the biggest understanding of what Nigel was doing. 'At the beginning of the band, he sort of instilled a kind of boot camp mentality that, to a certain extent, I think was needed,' he said.

As for the outfits – 'Nigel had the idea that we had to be quite controversial,' said Jason. 'We should dress ludicrously. When I look back now, it *was* ludicrous. Bondage gear and chains and Lycra and all sorts of stuff.'

'A lot of gay clubs was where we started off,' said Mark. 'You know, we'd be in our dressing room and the guy would introduce, "Here they are, Take That!" And the song would start and we'd all be trying to get out of our dressing room.'

'We was, like, running through this crowd having our arses pinched, our front bits pinched, and trying to get to the stage – trying to push past everybody and almost missing the cue for the beginning of the song,' Howard added. With all that going on, it's hardly surprising that it had an effect on them, or that Robbie, who was only 16, would make jokes about being gay for so many years. Their first video was pretty clearly aimed at the gay market, too: 'I got my arse wiped off with a mop and loads of jelly as me and four of me mates lay on our fronts naked,' observed Robbie. 'And then we had codpieces and pit boots and Lycra, all-in-ones.'

More ancient footage emerged. The boys were pictured on *Wogan* and talking to Lorraine Kelly, who made the point that they were constantly being compared to New Kids on the Block. Then came the single 'Pray'. 'It was at that very point where people started to think... [to] take me seriously as a songwriter,' Gary said.

By this time, the antics that traditionally play a role in the life of a pop star had begun. 'Drugs and sex and the pop 'n' roll,' said Mark brightly. 'I suppose that's what we were. I think we all had our fair share of fun and sex and frolics.'

'I was naughty, you know? Everyone was naughty,' Howard chipped in. 'Everyone had a good time. We had our share.'

'I don't remember Nigel saying, "No sex." I only remember Nigel saying, "No full-time girlfriends,"' Jason explained.

But the fans' behaviour could be obsessive and

that was a shock to the boys. 'I've had fans come up to me in Manchester and say, "Hey, listen, tell Jason that there's this girl threatening if anybody kisses or touches Jason, she's gonna stab them,"' said Gary, displaying a rather wicked sense of humour. 'And you think, "Oh my God, that's the last time I kiss Jason."'

They all sounded slightly shell-shocked about the fans, if the truth be told. 'It was the things that they did,' said Howard. 'You know, write all over everything. Disturb the neighbours. Break things. Try pinching things out of your garden.'

'You're asleep at night and someone throws something at the window,' said Gary. 'There's girls out there singing "Could It Be Magic" till three in the morning.' But it went with the territory and everyone knew that.

Then came 'Relight My Fire' with Lulu, who was also interviewed for the programme. 'We recorded it,' she said, 'and they said if I didn't like it, it wouldn't go out. But, of course, it was great. It was so much fun to record.'

'Within an hour or so of her doing it, the label rang me,' said Nigel. 'And he went, "You were right. She's done a brilliant vocal and it works brilliantly."'

Lulu and Jason had been close, and both were

happy to talk about that, too. 'Yeah, we had a lovely, special relationship,' said Jason, although the party line was that it had not gone beyond a flirtation. 'I think Lulu was gracious enough to have... to make you feel like you're special with her. Yeah, I felt very close to Lulu for a period.'

'He was so handsome,' said Lulu. 'He had a lot of energy and he worked really hard onstage, Jason.'

'Did I give her one?' asked Jason. 'I don't remember. If I did, I don't remember. I'm a gentleman. If Lulu says I've given her one and she says I was great, that's fine by me.'

'I am not going to answer that,' Lulu said wisely. 'And that's my prerogative.'

As Take That mania grew, a huge amount of merchandising came out to take full advantage of it. 'You could get a Take That clock, Take That dolls, Take That stickers,' said Nigel. 'There was a Take That calendar. There was Mark and Robbie merchandise as well. T-shirts, scarves, books, all sorts of stationery. There was even a Take That cake, would you believe?'

The boys then discussed 'Back for Good', another defining moment in Take That's history, but also the point when real problems began to emerge. 'Come the time that I realised I couldn't be sacked, that was when he lost me,' Robbie confessed ruefully. 'You know, it was like, "I am now too powerful!" I think that was... there was a time when I went, "Right, I can't be sacked now. Let's do drugs."'

The strains and stresses were clearly beginning to take their toll, although it all came out slowly at first. 'There was a little bit more arguing in the band now,' said Mark. 'There was still a togetherness but... you know, the jokes that used to be quite light were actually a bit heavier now.'

Nigel was aware of it, too. 'In Germany, the very first MTV Awards from the Brandenburg Gate, I flew in there to find Robbie in bed, shivering, ill, 'cause he's been up all night with a certain international model, drinking champagne and taking cocaine,' he said.

'Robbie always wanted to be more or do more than what he was doing in the band,' said Jason. 'So he started to cause problems. Or, to rephrase that, he started to become a problem for us.'

'I was so depressed,' said Robbie. 'So depressed. And I was going back to my hotel in Manchester... and I'd just drink myself into oblivion. And I could just remember wailing like a banshee, uncontrollable, in my room by myself, downing a bottle of neat vodka. And I was nineteen, twenty.'

Mark, who was to develop problems of his own with alcohol, was sympathetic. 'Do you know, he hid it well, in a sense,' he said. 'At night after gigs, I'd have a bit of wine. Rob obviously had his bit of vodka. But I didn't see him… It wasn't like I saw him walking around backstage with a bottle of vodka or anything like that.'

'Didn't really ever take him that seriously, 'cause he didn't really wanna be taken that seriously,' said Gary. 'He was just the joker. The funny guy, you know?'

Robbie himself was totally honest about what had been going on. 'My drug-taking would have happened with or without Take That,' he said. 'Before Take That, I'd done acid and speed and smoked a lot of weed. So I was sort of heading into that direction anyway.'

And so, as the whole world knows, Robbie left. For all the bitterness that ensued, Nigel was surprisingly rueful about it. 'The day that Robbie left was probably the hardest day ever, in all my professional career,' he said.

'Something just snapped inside my head,' Robbie said. 'I'd gone. I'd physically and mentally gone. I remember the night before, we went out with a competition winner for a curry. And then I went back to my hotel in Manchester, drank myself stupid again, woke up the next day, rehearsed as normal for the morning.'

'Robbie wasn't pulling his weight,' said Jason. 'He was just being quite belligerent really.'

With hindsight, everyone realised they had handled it very badly. 'We did it all wrong, I think,' said Gary. 'We sat there as a pack, like a gang. Told him what we thought of him. That he needed to pull his weight. What's he gonna do? He completely went on the defensive. Just sort of, completely, like, "Listen, if you want me to leave, I'll go." I was shocked. We were all shocked, I think. We didn't think he'd actually go.'

Howard, who had been hit hardest by the break-up of the band, was not impressed. 'We found out he was on a boat in the south of France, I think, with Paula Yates and George Michael,' he said. 'We thought, "Well, that's it. That's how much he gives a shit."' In reality, Robbie was devastated – but there was no turning back.

Only Jason was a little unmoved. 'When Robbie left, I didn't feel that much,' he said. 'For whatever reason, Robbie and I didn't get on that well in the band.'

CHAPTER ELEVEN

THE FEUDING BEGINS

Now the feuding between Robbie and Nigel Martin-Smith began, and they didn't play it down for the documentary. 'Nigel,' said Robbie flatly. 'Haven't got a nice word to say about him. He's definitely in the top three most disturbed individuals that I've ever worked with.'

Nigel wasn't taking that lying down. 'Well, what have I done?' he asked. 'What did I do, Rob? I took you out of Stoke-on-Trent. God, there's one thing I did for him. And I made him massive, and look at him now. Look where he is now.'

'He thought I could do a job,' said Robbie. 'You know, it wasn't a charitable event. There was no, "We'll pick him from Stoke and Tunstall 'cause he looks as though he needs it." I made him money. And he would say, "Yeah, I picked him and I don't get any credit for that." He picked me because I was good.'

'I gave him his career, as far as I'm concerned,' said Nigel, with a certain amount of justification.

'If it hadn't been him who'd found me, it'd have been somebody else,' said Robbie.

'Rubbish,' said Nigel. 'I mean, I've heard Robbie has been referring to the various members of Take That as "casualties from Take That". Robbie Williams, from the life of seventeen, has travelled the world first class, stayed in hotels. He's worth millions. He's a very lucky young lad. Don't talk to me about casualties, Robbie – it's sick.'

And then, perhaps, came the nub of the matter. 'I only wanted him to love me,' said Robbie. 'You know, that's the sad, really sad thing. I only wanted him to love me. And he never did.'

The boys really were prepared to talk about everything and that included the feud between Robbie and Gary. In truth, it was now all but over but Robbie couldn't resist having a go. 'Gary Barlow's a wanker!' he said. 'No, I'm joking. Maybe I can put some... Don't put that in ... 'Cause I'd wake up and I couldn't start the day or do the day without probably downing a bottle of vodka before the afternoon had finished. There was no plan.

Obviously in the back of my mind, it was, "Right, start a solo career, be big." I remember, at the time genuinely, genuinely thinking he's a genuinely crap songwriter.'

And then came 'Angels'. 'I think the biggest problem with Robbie [versus] Gary is that we were both trying to do the same thing,' said Gary, 'and only one person can win, really. It ['Angels'] is a great song. A great song. All the stars aligned for him, and… yeah, it worked out for him. It did. I was dropped by RCA. I didn't have a record deal. I couldn't get away from the industry quick enough. I just wanted to hide. Hide me somewhere because it was very humiliating, a lot of it. I've never laid in bed wishing I was Robbie Williams but, I guess seven or eight years ago, I lay in bed wishing I had his career. Definitely. I didn't wanna be something I wasn't. Maybe I should have been. Maybe I should've tried that.'

And so the boys began to talk about the present day, and here the documentary became really revealing. To a certain extent, everyone already knew the story, but what they all did next was not so well known. With the exception of Robbie, they had been out of the limelight for a decade now and there was real curiosity about how they'd all coped.

First to speak was Mark, who talked about his

beautiful Lake District home. 'We finished in Amsterdam and I came home and went on a two-week holiday,' he said. 'And I came to the Lakes. It was somewhere I'd always wanted to visit. I'd never visited here before. And I came up and had a beautiful time. Very relaxing. I knew all the other lads were gonna move to south Manchester, to the Cheshire area. And I didn't want it to become like the Take That village, where we all lived within a stone's throw of each other. I just wanted to get away from the whole thing. Why? I think that you live... I'd spent five or six years on the road with them, so I could think of nothing worse than living on the next street to them. In a sense. I think what was one of the weirdest things was to go from having your day-by-day schedule – you knew exactly what you were doing, exactly where you were going – to then just closing the gates and going, "OK, what do I do now?"'

With that, Mark began playing the piano and talking about the future, although what was actually about to happen was not what he was talking about at all. 'This is a song that I'm working on at the moment for a film, you know?' he said. 'I got a publishing deal this year, which is fantastic. I never had a publishing deal for so long. I miss Rob not being in my life like he was then. He's probably the one I miss the most. I missed him from when he left and I miss him being a close friend. I do still miss Rob.'

Then it was Howard's turn. 'I recorded my own album, which is, in my eyes, a great album,' he said. '[It's] just that we didn't end up releasing the album and that all went to pieces. It was an amazing single. It really was an amazing single. It was called "Speak Without Words". But it never got released. I get a buzz out of DJing so much. I love DJing, I really do. Ten years' time, I'd like to think that I was a successful house producer.'

And with that, the cameras moved to Bournemouth, where Howard was planning on living. 'This is my house, which hopefully is gonna be ready in about six weeks but, looking at it, I'm not so sure,' he said. 'I split up with me girlfriend and she moved here with my daughter and so, wherever my daughter goes, I go. So I decided to move round here – sell my other house and move here. That's the reason. Been going back and forward to Germany, 'cause me daughter lives in Germany as well. It's difficult to get things moving. And every time I come back, I want things changing and I can't follow what work's going on, and it's a bit of a nightmare, really.'

If the truth be told, it was Jason who had done the least since the split. 'Since the break up nearly ten years ago, I've gone back to college,' he said. 'Did some college courses. I did some backpacking. Travelled the world. I've sat around a lot, pondering a lot. Chilled out a lot. Yeah, so now I'm thirty-five, I'm just starting now to feel like I would like to go back and do something. But I'm not sure... I'm not sure what yet.

'I've been sleeping poorly for, like... I'd say fifteen years actually. There was never too much of a problem during Take That but it was always there, present. But it's since Take That, so in the last ten years, my sleep's just gotten awful. I just have phases where I just can't sleep. I've analysed it for myself and I think, what it is, what happens to me as I lie down and I'm absolutely exhausted, something else kicks in. It's like another... not a voice. I do have voices in me head but it's not one of those voices. Something just kicks in which... It almost challenges me. A stubbornness coming from somewhere inside of myself. Stopping myself from getting a decent night's sleep. It's almost like... something in me wants to will me to fail.'

Gary also welcomed the cameras into his lovely home, then in Cheshire. 'Good day, everyone, and welcome to my crib,' he said to the cameras. 'Come on in. When I bought this place, it was a total wreck. This is one of those lounges that you never sit in, like, ever. This is the second time in ten years I've ever been in here. It's great. Anyone fancy any dinner? Thank you. Have you been messing with my chairs? Hello, gorgeous [to his daughter]. I've got my computer in here. This is where I do all my work. Dawn was one of the dancers. I was seventeen, she was eighteen.'

Finally, in front of the cameras, the group met again – the first time the four of them had been together in ten years. Although Robbie was still absent – that final part of the reunion was still to come – it was a very emotional time with far-reaching consequences.

'It's gonna be interesting to see how everyone looks and how everyone... what everyone's done with their lives in the last ten years,' said Gary.

'It's actually great to be getting all together, all in one room, and I think it's gonna be a bit of a mash-up tonight,' said Howard.

'I think everybody would love Rob to come,' said Mark. 'It has been ten years now for us all. I think it's... and I think they'd all really like to see him.'

'I'll be pleased to see him and I think he will come,' said Jason. 'I hope he does come. If he doesn't, I think he'll miss out. It'll be nice to see him but it might also be a bit strange. I might wanna give him a slap. A cosh around his head for saying horrible things about Take That.'

In the event, Robbie didn't come. He was still such a massive solo star at that point that he might have felt it wasn't a good idea on those grounds – although, in one of those strange coincidences that fate lays on, just as the boys reunited, his own star began to fade.

Perhaps inevitably, given Robbie's absence, the reunited foursome's first topic of conversation seemed to be his departure from Take That and – less predictably – a sense that they had all somehow let him down. 'I think I was probably pretty instrumental in Robbie's leaving,' said Jason to Howard. 'I think I could've tried to persuade Robbie a bit more than I did to stay. I could've looked after him a bit more. But I think I just wanted to be on your side and against him so I felt more secure.'

'I remember Mark saying that nobody was really there for Robbie,' said Howard. 'And it's true, because I kind of realise now how young he was and what happened, and you don't really know what's going though his head. I didn't really... I did care but it just happened so fast and... I wish I'd said something.'

'I still feel bad about that day when Bob went,' said Gary, 'because I feel like we probably did it all wrong. I felt like we did all gang up one side of the table and say to him, "What you doing? What you doing? What's going on?" You know…'

'Why did we do that, do you think?' asked Jason.

'I think the reason why was… I don't think we were protecting Mark or Jay or Robbie,' said Gary. 'I think we were protecting Take That.'

'That's what we were,' said Mark. 'That's what, the last five years, we had been groomed to be. We were that band.'

It was at this point that the four of them were told that Robbie would not be joining them. All of them were clearly rather shocked. 'No… Well… I'm not surprised, to be honest,' said Mark, searching for a response. 'I think that it's… you know, we have, over the years, seen a bit of each other, haven't we? And, er… and it is ten years since Rob's been in this environment and… you know, you gotta… and I understand… that him not wanting to come… It's a shame.'

'I'm gutted that Robbie's not coming,' said Jason.

'Yeah, I'm gutted,' said Mark.

But Robbie had recorded a message for them, which was now played. 'Howard, you know, I… I

231

just sincerely apologise for any upset that I may have caused you after me leaving the band,' he said. 'Anything that I said, and anything that I've done subsequently that has been demeaning towards you, I apologise. You're never anything but nice to me, and you put me up in your house in Ashton, and we went round Ashton on Sunday night with you and your mate... And I thank you very much for the love you showed me.

'To Jay – I'm really sorry as well about taking the piss when I was in the band and when I left, and I think you're a good man and I'd love to see you one day. Mark... well, we're still in touch and we speak to each other. I think you're a genius, mate, and the nicest person I've ever met. Gaz... you're an amazing songwriter. I apologise for saying that you weren't. I had my head up my arse at the time and wanted to be in Oasis; I apologise. You are an amazing songwriter and you have an amazing voice.'

Robbie might not have been there in person, but it was done. The feud was at an end. The long-awaited start to reforming Take That could begin at last.

CHAPTER TWELVE

THE BOYS ARE BACK IN TOWN

The response to the documentary was phenomenal. Nearly a decade after Take That had split up, none of its members had had any idea whether anyone would be interested in watching a documentary about what they'd been up to over the past ten years, less still seeing them on stage again. But the documentary was met with a massive wave of affection, interest and a desire to see them perform. Talks about a tour began and, to be honest, some of them could have used the money. Gary had made an awful lot the first time round; the others rather less, and their workloads had not been that heavy of late.

Initially, they weren't sure but it wasn't long before they were tempted, with or without Robbie. 'Robbie has been included in the offer but I don't know what he thinks,' said Gary. 'But we would do it without him. I think we'd have to. Financially it's a very tempting idea and I know a lot of our fans would like it. Our live shows were what made Take That great so, if we came back, it would have to beat that, otherwise I wouldn't want to do it.'

A press conference was hastily convened although, as always, it was marked by the absence of You Know Who. 'Thank you very much for giving us the last ten years off but, unfortunately, the rumours are true ... Take That are going back on tour!' cried Gary. The fans were euphoric, but it was a risk. After Robbie had left, they'd tried to make a go of it as a foursome and it hadn't worked. Would they be able to pull it off now?

Then there was the unresolved Robbie situation. What would he make of it all? 'The door's always open for Rob,' said Mark resolutely. 'If ever he's bored one day and we're on the road and he wants to come and sing a song, we're always ready to do that. We'll have a spare mic ready for him on stage.'

And as for the boys themselves, how would they cope? Take That did not just sing: they were a troupe of very able dancers, whose on-stage antics had become the stuff of pop legend. Now they were all in their late 30s: how on earth would they manage those acrobatics now? 'Last week, we sat and watched some of the old videos and I felt exhausted just watching them... I've promised I'll cut down on the cigarettes,' said Mark.

At the same time that the documentary was airing, the boys released a compilation of hits, *Never Forget – The Ultimate Collection*, which did very well and helped to soothe fears that the public wasn't interested in them any more. Plans for a tour, the 'Ultimate Tour', were announced for the following year, although there was still a great deal of nervousness about how this would pan out. Would anyone actually want to see them perform again? They needn't have worried.

'We really didn't plan to get this response, especially with the tour,' said Gary. 'We were a bit nervous about whether tickets would sell. I had my phone off when they went on sale and then, when I turned it on, I had all these messages about selling out all the dates in five minutes and would we agree to release more dates? It was just amazing – it really is overwhelming!'

Not that they were going to overdo it: this was dipping a toe in the water to see how it would go. Eleven dates had been arranged in the UK and

Ireland but these sold out so quickly that the number of performances had to be doubled. The fans couldn't buy tickets fast enough: the full 275,000 were sold in less than 3 hours, making it the 2nd-fastest sell-out tour of 2005. (The fastest was, yes, Robbie's.) Stadiums were added to the list of venues: so many people wanted to see them that other places were judged to be simply too small.

The sold-out tour was everything the boys had been hoping it would be, and more. They were supported by Pussycat Dolls and the Sugababes when they were in Ireland; Beverley Knight stood in for Lulu on 'Relight My Fire' – Lulu herself appeared during the stadium shows for 'Relight My Fire' and 'Never Forget' – and it was as if they had never been away. Such was the euphoria surrounding Take That's return to the scene that, in May 2006, when the tour ended, they signed a £3 million deal with Polydor and released a comeback album, *Beautiful World*. It entered the charts at UK No 1; to date, it has sold more than 2.6 million records in the UK and is the 35th best-selling album in UK music history.

The boys and their fans couldn't have been happier and part of this was because there had been some fairly significant changes from what had gone before. There had been a number of reasons that they'd originally split, and it wasn't all because Robbie had left. Yes, they'd been living in each other's pockets for years and wanted a change but, the first time round, it had been all about Gary. He was seen as the talent in the band, with the others just backing him up, and this was no longer going to be the case. All of them were going to be credited as co-writers from now on, which meant they would all share the publishing royalties, rather than Gary getting the lion's share. It was to be a much more equal set-up and everyone, Gary included, seemed much happier that way.

From that moment on, there was no stopping them. 'Patience', their first single in ten years, was released in November 2006 and went straight to UK No 1. Gary, who had just published his autobiography, appeared on Jonathan Ross's TV chat show. A new website was launched. The boys appeared on Chris Moyles' show on Radio 1. They won Best Live Return at the Vodafone Awards. Suddenly they were all over the media that had ignored them for so long: in November, they made the cover of both *Attitude* and *Q* magazine and featured in the *Telegraph*'s Saturday magazine. A DVD of the 'Ultimate Tour' was released: it, too, went straight to UK No 1. They appeared at the Pride of Britain awards. They were everywhere.

Given that a year earlier, most of them would have had trouble getting arrested, the sheer scale of the comeback was quite remarkable. Take That began making plans to tour Europe; in the meantime, they were all over the airwaves, being interviewed as much as having their music played. One minute they were with Johnny Vaughan on Capital; the next with Jo Whiley on Radio 1's *Live Lounge*. In the run-up to the release of *Beautiful World*, they did a showcase performance in front of 300 people at London's Abbey Road studios, which was subsequently broadcast on BBC2. People simply couldn't get enough.

The boys themselves could hardly believe what was happening. In an interview several years later, referring to that phenomenal time, Jason said, 'Being a good pop band is not just about good pop songs. It's about a good story. Our story is pretty good.'

It certainly was. 'It's an unbelievable journey,' said Gary. 'It's a script you wouldn't believe.' It was that, too.

It didn't hurt that no one had a bad word to say about them. They had been popular not just among fans, but among people who actually knew them and that fund of goodwill was pouring out now. 'They are lovely, lovely people,' said Mark Frith, who edited *Smash Hits* during Take That's first incarnation. 'Unaffected. Ordinary. I first met them when they came into the office and made tea for us, around the time of the first single. I remember Mark and Gary walking round the office with pieces of paper with everyone's milk and sugar requirements noted down. It was great tea, proper northern tea.'

'In an industry full of snakes, con artists, sleazeballs and fakes, they shine out as a bastion of old-fashioned decency, respect and talent,' said Piers Morgan.

Alex James of Blur also had good words to say. 'We first encountered them at a TV show before Blur or Take That were famous,' he said. 'We were all moody and hungover and, "Who are these prancing puppet doinks?" But they were all really smiley and soft and wide-eyed and irresistibly pleasant. There is a theory that they were incredibly nice to absolutely everybody and some of the runners and researchers they were nice to are now running things and were more than happy to give them a helping hand when they needed it ... It's the triumph of nice. Bravo.'

With the distance of a decade, the boys were now more able to look back on the whole extraordinary story with some understanding. They still seemed a bit bemused about the madness of the early days. 'I just never understood why they were all always... screaming,' said Howard. 'And they were so young – fourteen, thirteen, twelve and just... screaming. I thought it was... stupid, really. And Mark had the most fans, and that really didn't make any sense. Didn't understand that one...'

Mark was asked if they were selling sex. 'Yeah,' he said rather reluctantly. 'Or, erm... I didn't... see it, in that way, then. We were sexual. We had a lot of energy and it was a great feeling. I didn't look at it as... what's the word? As calculated. As cynical. As "selling sex". Now, though, when you look at it... At the time, I thought we were just having a laugh. But Jay will probably stand here for an hour and talk about, were we selling sex? He'd love it.'

The success of Take That was so great that other groups wondered if they could do something similar. Ronan Keating was openly speculating about a reunion for Boyzone – and, indeed, it happened. 'We're very aware of how good Take That are, and know we have to be on a par with them,' he said. 'There won't be a flat, boring stage. We're all dancing again and learning different things we've never done before to rival their pole-dancing and stuff.'

The madness was well and truly under way again. When *Beautiful World* was released, the boys held two signing sessions, in London and Manchester. Fans queued overnight to get to see them. Many were fans from the old days, too. 'We have waited ten years for this,' said Caryn Webb, 43, from Croydon, Surrey. 'Once a Take That fan, always a Take That fan.'

Lisa Vale, 26, from Dagenham, and Yasmin Johnson, 18, sisters from Hornchurch in Essex, thought so, too. 'You don't think about the cold when you know what you're going to get at the end of it,' said Lisa. 'It's been freezing but I think the adrenaline kept me going.'

'It was absolutely amazing,' agreed Yasmin.

'I'd do it again in a heartbeat,' said Rachel Grant, 24, from London. 'I took three days off school when the band broke up. I was devastated.'

Television wanted them, too. They did *An Audience With Take That*. The album and single were both at UK No 1, something they had never managed to achieve, even in the old days. 'Can't believe how good this year's been and the single and album at No 1 is like a dream come true,' said Howard. 'We're well made up. No 1s the same week!'

'It's like winning the Premiership and the Champions League in the same year because it's been eleven years and the first we've all written together, it makes it extra special,' said Mark.

'It's just amazing,' said Gary. 'I never dreamed this could happen. If you'd have told me this fourteen months ago, [that] we'd have a No 1 album and single in the same week, our first ever, I'd have never have believed you. It's like a fairy tale. Totally brilliant.'

'It's the strangest thing in the world eleven years on to have this happen,' said Jason. 'It really feels like we've achieved something and for me it's a testament to good friendship and the hard work we've all put in. It feels really special and we're all really made up.'

In fact, the situation was even better than they realised: they were also top of the download charts, thus occupying three top slots. The following week they made musical history: occupying the UK No 1 chart slot for single, album, download of single, download of album and DVD for *The Ultimate Tour*. They also drew in the highest audience for the *An Audience With...* show in two years.

'Patience' was eventually knocked off the top by *X Factor* winner Leona Lewis but, even there, the boys were in on the act – they accompanied her on 'A Million Love Songs' just before she won the show.

If 2006 had been good, 2007 just got better. As the year kicked off, *Beautiful World* was still at UK No 1 and there was talk about staging *Take That – The Musical*. While the boys were not due to star in it, in the wake of *Mamma Mia* – the hugely successful stage show built around ABBA songs – there was a huge amount of interest in doing something similar with the music of another band – and who better than Take That? They were almost as popular as ABBA and, with a solid back catalogue of songs, they were ripe for the picking.

The musical did eventually get staged, but the boys themselves were not happy about it – so much so that they put out a statement to that effect. 'There have been reports in the press today about a Take That musical,' it read. 'The band would like to state categorically that this production is being undertaken with neither their involvement nor their endorsement. They would wish their fans and the general public to know that this production is absolutely and a hundred per cent nothing to do with Take That.'

Towards the end of January, their next single, 'Shine', was released. Nothing illustrated the new team-based approach more than this single and its hugely entertaining accompanying video. For a start, the lead singer was Mark. The video, as enjoyable as anything they had ever put out, was intended to resemble a Busby Berkeley musical dance number and it did. It kicked off with Mark, in top hat and tails – though sans tie – on a never-ending staircase, with Howard and Jason sitting on the steps below. Gary is at the very bottom of the steps playing the piano. Gradually, hordes of dancers join them as the music reaches a crescendo. It was as good as anything they'd done but, this time, all of them could bask in the glory, rather than just Gary getting all the praise. 'Shine' eventually got to UK No 1, their tenth time at the top.

A tour had already been confirmed for Europe but now the rest of the world wanted in on the act. The boys went off to stay for three days in Taiwan, where they were mobbed. 'So many fans have come to the airport. I am very surprised and want to say hi to my mum,' quipped Howard. While they were there, it was Mark's birthday: the fans sang 'Happy Birthday', much to his delight.

In February, Take That received further recognition that they were back in the game, when 'Patience' won Best Single in the Brit Awards. It was still in the Top

20, as was 'Shine', which meant the boys had two songs there at once. They continued to tour: when more dates were announced, phone lines jammed and websites crashed as fans rushed to buy tickets. The boys were also continuing their promotional appearances around the world, now getting to Japan and Australia, and proving a sensation wherever they went.

CHAPTER THIRTEEN

SING WHEN YOU'RE WINNING

When you're winning, you're winning. *An Audience With Take That* won the top award at the British Academy of Film and Television Awards. They were nominated in ITV's Greatest Living Britons 2007 poll. There was another single – 'I'd Wait for Life', the third from *Beautiful World*. It only reached UK No 14 but this was because the band had decided to take a rest rather than embark on heavy promotional activities. But it didn't matter – they were on such a roll that nothing could have got in their way.

They were certainly very much in demand, appearing at the Concert for Diana alongside Elton John, Tom Jones, Italian tenor Andrea Bocelli, Donny Osmond, Jason Donovan and many more.

'Introduced by David Beckham, closing with "Back for Good" – does it get any better than this?' asked the *Mirror*. 'The Take That boys sparked a mass sing-along as the penultimate act of the night. And they had jetted in especially from their hols to take part. Gotta hand it to 'em.' The *Sun* pointed out to David Beckham that he strongly resembled Gary Barlow, due to his new haircut. 'It's my new look,' said Becks.

Yet it was also very different from the old days. Apart from the fact that it was so much more of a joint endeavour, they were branching out in many different ways, now recording the theme, 'Rule the World', for the film *Stardust*, co-written and directed by *Lock, Stock...* producer Matthew Vaughn. That led to an invitation to perform at the first ever National Movie Awards, yet another sign of the band's widespread appeal.

Take That weren't just popular, they were also becoming cool, something they had never been in their heyday. In the autumn of 2007, they were chosen to model for Marks and Spencer's 'Autograph' collection, a campaign that was to be shot by the noted photographer Rankin. While M&S might not be the last word in cutting-edge fashion, it only chose stars with massive popular appeal: Twiggy and Myleene

Klass were among those who had modelled for the store in the past.

Global demand was now such that the boys sold out their 'Beautiful World' tour, which started in November 2007, and garnered sensational reviews from the press. An appearance on *Friday Night with Jonathan Ross* followed, in which appreciative screaming began from the audience before Ross had even got round to announcing the band. 'A mop for aisle three,' he quipped, before introducing 'the greatest boy band of all time' – and commenting that that was stretching the definition of 'boy' to the very limit. In the backroom, the boys grinned affably. Although indisputably heartthrobs, they had become something else now, too – national treasures.

They were pretty good-humoured national treasures, too. They took the most intense ribbing from Ross, especially Gary. Ross praised him for his weight loss, while telling him that everyone used to feel sorry for him for being the least good-looking member of the band. 'Now you're the best looking,' he added, as the rest of them laughed it off. He then solicitously enquired as to how their knees were holding up on tour.

Ross didn't let up, talking about how they managed to breakdance at such an advanced age and pointing out that, when the backing dancers gave the boys an on-stage lap dance, one of those dancers was Dawn, Gary's wife, and the person she was giving the lap dance to was Howard, not Gary. 'I can go on a long time,' said Howard affably. 'I trust them,' said Gary. 'And we thought it would be a bit much if it were me.'

The biggest difference between now and then, though, came through in the fact that they were all older and considerably more in charge of their own destiny. 'It was our whole life last time – we didn't have time for anything else,' said Gary. 'But we do have other lives now – it's only half our life. We're in control now and it's nice to be in control of your own destiny.'

Inevitably, the subject of Robbie rejoining them came up. There were whoops from the audience at the thought of it, although Ross couldn't resist observing that the boys' body language clearly showed they all tightened up at the mere mention of it. They sounded calm enough when they spoke, however. Jason, whom Jonathan accused of grinding his jaw when the possibility was mentioned, confessed that he had been the most hopeful that Robbie would come back, but added, 'Why should he? He's doing all right on his own.' But was the door still open, were Robbie to choose to do so? 'Always,' said Gary, which brought the house down once more.

The sheer scale of what they'd accomplished was evident in the boys' disbelief at what had happened over the past two years. 'There's not a night on stage when there's not a moment when we look at each other and it's like, "What are we still doing here?"' said Jason. The reunion, which had initially been seen as a toe-dipping exercise, had now been going on for two years and, far from showing any signs of abating, their popularity was growing all the time.

Could they have been any better sports? Ross made them watch a spoof of the reunion, from Star Stories, in which a fake Gary drives up in a clapped-out old banger to find the others living in a skip; they comment on how thin he is and explain that they have to live like this as the royalties have dried up. Initially, they turn down his request for a reunion, before the fake Mark says, 'Only kidding, Gary, we're fucking starving!' Jason (the real one) was heard to observe, morosely, that the spoof was remarkably close to what actually happened.

The subject of M&S modelling came up, too: 'Looking good in the cheaper clothes,' said Jonathan, before hastily adding, 'Reasonably priced.' They got to keep the clobber, the band agreed, before Mark whispered that they even got a discount card, too – 'fifty per cent.' 'But that's only on clothes, not food,' said Howard. 'They don't want old Tubby to fall off the wagon,' said Jonathan cruelly, but Gary took it in good part.

The audience reaction was indicative of the mood of the nation: everyone was just so pleased to see them together again. Meanwhile, although Jason was right that Robbie was doing well and certainly never had to work again if he didn't want to, there were signs that he was faltering. His career was not quite as stratospheric as it had been when the boys had been languishing in the wilderness, and eccentricities were beginning to emerge. Robbie was very keen on the subject of UFOs and, increasingly, it was this pursuit, rather than any great career success, that was coming to dominate his share of the headlines. Their paths were edging closer together – it just wasn't obvious yet how close.

All those remarks about the boys being older, though, were not totally wide of the mark. In October 2007, Howard, by then 39, was rushed to hospital when it emerged that he'd suffered a collapsed lung after a particularly energetic bout of dancing on stage. He managed to get through the rest of the performance but was then told he would have to rest. Howard professed himself willing to defy doctor's orders but the band insisted he must put himself first. For a brief period, they performed as a trio, although Howard did bring the house down in Vienna, when he appeared on stage in a medical gown. After reading out a speech in German apologising for his non-appearance, he turned and walked off, revealing that the medical gown was open at the back – and that he was wearing nothing underneath. On another occasion, he appeared in drag, again making a statement in German about how much he wanted to appear. It was, said Jason, 'typically Howard to make light of a bad situation'. He certainly did as much as he could, appearing regularly at the beginning of the shows to introduce the rest of the band and attempting, at the very least, to make his presence felt.

Before long, the band were able to put out a statement. 'Everyone, I'm sure, will be pleased to hear that Howard is making a speedy recovery and the doctors are very happy with his progress,' it read. 'He will, as a result, be rejoining his bandmates in Hamburg on Wednesday this week when the tour arrives there. Although it is still not clear when he will be back on stage performing with the other guys, the early indications are that it will be very soon. Howard was discharged from Hospital in Vienna on Saturday afternoon and is currently resting with his family. Mark, Gary and Jason all visited Howard after the show in Vienna on Friday night along with the dancers and musicians to help cheer him up. They're all looking forward to him joining them this week in Germany.'

Howard was also getting himself noticed off stage. It was, by now, well known that Take That had been nothing like as squeaky clean as their earlier image had suggested but now he went much further. 'Cannabis should be legalised,' he said. 'If more people went out stoned than drunk, I think there would be less fighting, less trouble and less violence.' Predictably, his remarks caused outrage: Howard was, after all, a role model. But the fuss soon blew over and a fully recovered Howard joined the rest of the boys on stage once more.

'Rule the World' (Take That's film theme) now went into the charts at UK No 2 as the 'Beautiful World' tour broke one record after another. It was a sell-out in all the countries it visited, the tickets for the 49 shows selling out within 40 minutes of being announced. Even Howard's injury didn't spoil matters: not a single date was cancelled as the fans cheered them on from one number to the next.

The tour did drain them in some ways, but the boys knew how lucky they were. 'We've done twenty-eight dates in Europe and being away from home for a long time is tough,' Gary told the *Sun*. 'You miss your family a lot. Luckily, my wife Dawn is on tour with us but you do miss the kids like mad. My daughter is too young to understand. Christmas is just around the corner – it's not easy for the lads fighting in Afghanistan and Iraq. It makes you realise how lucky we are. I am a workaholic. I can't imagine ever stopping writing songs. I've only written one song for someone else this year – Katherine Jenkins – which has done really well. I'll do more of that in the future but we are all writing for Take That. People keep emailing me, asking if I have another "Patience" tucked away. Believe me, if I did, it would be tucked away for our next album.'

Mark agreed. 'It's great to be home,' he said. 'It was getting to the point where we were on autopilot, but being back has given us all a lift. London is a brilliant place. My house is only just around the corner from the hotel and coming to the gig like this every night is a bit special.'

They seemed more mature now, too. For all the showbiz glitz, none of the boys were being reckless: they had been there before, seen it all and knew it could disappear tomorrow. They had social consciences, too. 'I have always been quite wise with my money,' said Jason. 'I never splashed out on Aston Martins or a Ferrari or anything like that. I've got my money in a Manchester investment firm who only get involved with ethical projects. I want my money to go into wind power and renewable energy. Everything has to be Fair Trade or operate an ethical practice. It means a lot to me. When I was younger it was all about trying to double and treble my money but, this time round, it's more important to me that the money is making a difference at the same time.'

Jason was still single (and still is at the time of writing) but was adamant that he'd settle down one day. 'I still feel too young to get married,' he said. 'I really want to and I would love to have kids. At the moment, I like life the way it is and I don't want to do it just because I feel I have to while I'm young. I'm not as into shopping as the other lads. They are like girls. On tour, they've been coming back to the hotel with bags and bags of new clothes. I'm a northern lad – all I need is a good jacket and I'm happy.'

All the boys sounded euphoric. Just a couple of

years earlier, it would have been unimaginable for them to be in their current position: now they were on top of the world.

CHAPTER FOURTEEN

THE CIRCUS

Can a tour ever have been as aptly named as the one Take That were to embark on next? The palaver surrounding them was as great as ever and, truly, life was a circus wherever they went. On top of that, they had set themselves such high standards that it was hard work to surpass them – but surpass them they did. Unlike the vast majority of boy bands who implode, they had not only been given a second chance but had a whole new lease of life. They were, however, going to take some time during 2008 to do their own thing. One of the main lessons learned the first time round was that work could be exhausting. They didn't want to push themselves so hard any more, not least because they all had lives outside the band.

'My regrets about re-forming are... absolutely none,' said Mark to one interviewer, 'except I would have loved for Rob to have come and done it with us. He should be here, having a cup of tea. Having a laugh. The good thing, though, is that, originally, I wanted him to come back so that we could make something right, something that had been wrong. Back in the past. But I think we've done that now. Really, all Take That is, is a therapy session. One long therapy session.'

Bridges were being repaired now in a big way. Hostilities had ceased, both sides were dropping one hint after another that the band might re-form, and Robbie's increasing happiness in his personal life meant that many of the stresses and strains of the past had disappeared. Occasional meetings took place behind the scenes, and speculation in the press that they would all get back together never went away.

Everyone seemed happier in the newly democratic Take That. Gary was still probably the most musically talented, but everyone was getting their time in the limelight and it was working much better that way. Howard and Jason, while easily the best dancers, had not had their fair share of lead vocals in the past and that was being remedied now. Jason, in particular, was now getting the opportunity to do far more than he had done – not least because a lack of self-belief had held him back in the past. He now sang lead on '84', the b-side to the new single 'Up All Night'.

'I didn't have confidence in myself, so it didn't happen then,' Jason said, referring to the first incarnation. 'There wasn't enough encouragement from the others to change my lack of confidence. I was consigned to doing backing vocals and dance routines. That was my job description at the time.'

To be fair, a lot of this had been down to Nigel Martin-Smith, who'd had a very clear idea of exactly what he wanted when he put the band together. 'Nigel had his vision of how things would be and that's how they were,' said Jason. 'We pretty much all fell in line with his vision. It was frustrating. That's human nature. I was with a bunch of lads and wanted to prove myself in among them. Although we are all friends and care for each other, there is a rivalry we all share. You always want to appeal to the people around you. I was frustrated. I'm sure all the lads were, in their own way. It's why we are doing what we are doing. We want to prove things to ourselves.'

But he was very pleased that he'd been the lead

singer on the new number – because the decision was not theirs alone. The record company had had a say in it and, if they'd been concerned that Jason wasn't up to it, he wouldn't have been allowed to sing. 'I like it for that reason,' said Jason. 'It's only the third time I've done a lead on a Take That song. It is a rarity. We're trying to be more democratic across the board. As far as the songwriting is concerned, we are all contributing more than ever. Likewise with who gets to sing what. I am probably the weakest – well, not probably, I *am* the weakest singer in the band!'

The song itself was a nostalgic one, harking back to the 1980s – a time Jason said that he was at his happiest, although it did mention the war in Iraq as well. 'It is semi-autobiographical,' he said. 'That stuff happened and the facts of the miners' strike are there. I wanted a staccato rhythm and to tell a story, and we decided to tell a nostalgic one. It's a story from my childhood. Back then, I was breakdancing on the corner of the street with my lino on the ground and my breakdance crew. We were just kids. I was fourteen or fifteen years old. I look back with huge fondness. [But] we don't want to be a protest band. It wasn't written for that reason. I wanted to make reference of the fact the Conservatives were in power and go on to sing about what happened with Iraq. That and the fact Iraq rhymed with "heart attack" from the first line. It doesn't express opinions about things back then. It makes statements of what's happened. It is quite innocent in that way.'

The DVD for the 'Beautiful World' tour was released: it went straight in at UK No 1. They scooped up a couple of Brits as the awards began to pile up again, including an Ivor Novello award for 'Shine'. True to their word, though, the boys continued their solo activities as well. Howard had built up a large following in his own right as a DJ and was back on the road again in a break between tours. Gary continued to make solo appearances and run his music publishing company.

Mark and Emma, meanwhile, were expecting their second child, and Gary and Dawn their third. Indeed, he sent out a very happy message about it: 'Dawn and me are pregnant again! And before you ask, it was all planned. Funny, everyone asks us if it was a mistake. I guess we've waited quite a long time now, with Emily being six this year. Anyway, we can't wait. It's due three days before my birthday! It's also quite nice because Mark's new baby is due in December we're sharing stories already. Most of the young baby stuff I've forgotten now, so he's being a good source of info.' Take That – well, some of them at any rate – had settled down.

But such was the momentum that had built up over the past couple of years that no one wanted to stay away too long. So, still in the spring of 2008, much earlier than anticipated, talks began about a new Take That album. As the year moved on, it was announced that 'Greatest Day' would be their next single and, in September, they won the Sony Ericsson Tour of the Year for their 'Beautiful World' marathon, but it was in October that the heaviest hints of what was to come really appeared.

The band had a new album on the way: *The Circus*. Artwork for the cover was released: it showed the four of them on high wires with a blue sky in the background, a very apt image for all that they had been through. Balancing on the tightrope against all the odds – it was a precursor to one of the greatest tours of all.

The boys knew how lucky they were and wanted to give something back. To that end, they established the Take That Trust, which was to bestow grants to projects within education/training/medicine/health/sickness. This was a serious endeavour. Increasingly, it was the case that, when one of the boys had a birthday, the fans were encouraged to make donations to charities instead of sending presents. This was a way of channelling these donations into a central trust, one that the boys could be sure was being administered properly. It was also a mark of how far they'd come: from teenybop sensation, which no one had expected to last, to durable and highly regarded entertainers, determined to do their bit and give something back to a world that had treated them extremely well.

When tickets for the next tour, 'The Circus', were put on sale towards the end of October, they sold out in five hours, earning Take That a place in history for the fastest-selling tour in the UK. It broke the previous record, held by Michael Jackson's 'Bad' tour in 1987. Such was the demand for tickets that two more dates were added: at Manchester's Old Trafford Cricket Ground and London's Wembley Stadium. Take That were staggered, as well they might have been. 'We are, once again, totally astounded by the response today and amazed at being able to break such records,' they said in a statement. 'We feel very privileged to be in this position at such a time. We're all meeting up this afternoon to start planning next summer and promise to make it the very best show we've ever done. See you in 2009!'

Everyone was determined to give it their all and, in

Gary's case, that had the extra dimension of rigid self-control when it came to maintaining his hunk status. 'I just can't control myself around food, if I'm honest,' he told one interviewer as a plate of salad arrived for lunch. 'Anything fatty or high-calorie is out. Mine is definitely a future without fries. In the studio, while making the album, the others would be dialling out late at night for burgers and chocolate while I'd be there with my tuna salad and protein bar, thinking, "This is shit!" I mean, look how thin they are. It isn't fair. But life isn't fair and, if this is what it's going to take for me to stay looking like this, I can cope with it.'

By his own admission, Jason had been very cautious about the reunion, but it had been a spectacular success. By a long way the quietest and most reflective of the boys, he was finally coming to terms with what fame meant and his own role within the band.

'I was wary, I admit,' he said. 'I'd not been wholly comfortable with the pop-star thing before. In fact, I'd fought it, thinking, "I'm more complex than that. It's not who or what I am." But that was just a silly fight I was having with myself. The people who care about this stuff want me to be a Take That person and there's nothing I can do about it. It doesn't have to represent my whole being. Realising that, I determined to relax and enjoy it more this time around.'

He was also enjoying spending time with the others: 'From that point of view, being in Take That is just the best thing ever. I wish everyone could experience it.'

It was that bonding between all of them that made the band what it was. 'There are many more talented individuals out there than me,' said Howard modestly. 'I don't have what it takes to shine on my own. But when you get the four of us together, there's a real magic, something people respond to. They see the friendship and commitment. Good songs, hard graft and chemistry – that's Take That.'

Gary, too, was keen to emphasise that they were far happier together than they had been before, as they all got to share the glory. 'In the old days, lead vocals were a sensitive issue, basically 'cause I wanted to do them all,' he said with commendable honesty. 'I was young, ambitious and selfish. Robbie was the first to challenge that, but hearing him would only make me want to try to do the same song better. My own insecurity issues, totally. I don't have them any more and, as a result, I'm enjoying letting everyone else have time in the sun.'

Ah, Robbie... The very fact that Gary was able to mention him so calmly in this context was a sign of how much everyone had mellowed and, by now, the boys really actively wanted him to return.

'It would be bloody brilliant if he came back some day,' said Mark, revealing that all of them had actually met Robbie in Los Angeles as they got ready for the tour. 'There's nothing missing without him in a musical sense, but still it would be so great. I think we'd all have Rob back tomorrow if he wanted it and the time felt right. For now, though, it's been just brilliant to have nights out with him again. We've had a right giggle. I'm really made up to be seeing him. I think we all are.'

In November, the boys played at the European Music Awards, a full 15 years after they'd done so the first time around. Then it was off to Paris to launch the new album. At St Pancras station, they gave an interview in which they were told that the new album was heralded as their best yet. 'We heralded it,' said Mark who, like the rest of them, had lost none of the charm that made them so well loved.

More records were broken. *The Circus* album was released and sold over 130,000 copies on the opening day. Not surprisingly, it ended up at UK No 1, their fifth album to do so, and stayed there long enough to become the first UK No 1 album of 2009.

But still the boys managed to maintain that balance between the personal and the professional, with Gary taking time out to take part in a charity climb up Mount Kilimanjaro in Tanzania. A number of other well-known faces were involved, but it was Gary's idea and it raised more than £1.3 million for Comic Relief. Everyone involved met the then Prime Minister Gordon Brown, who congratulated them on their efforts. 'It has been a privilege for the whole team to meet the Prime Minister today and under such special circumstances,' said Gary in a statement. 'To think that our efforts on the mountain and the incredible generosity of the public have inspired school children and have now been supported by the government is unbelievable. If the money raised can help control malaria and also help poor and vulnerable people in the UK, it will all have been worthwhile. What an unforgettable day.'

Meanwhile, critical reaction to the new album had been enormously positive. Coincidentally, Britney Spears had a new album out, also called *Circus* – as was her subsequent tour – and it was widely agreed that the boys had won that particular battle. 'We're pleased to report it's pretty damn amazing,' said the review on the BBC website. 'Modern-day Take That are like the drama faces of Melpomene and Thalia [the Greek muses of tragedy and comedy, respectively]. Gary Barlow, the graceful swan of the group, is cementing his position as the country's premier pop writer by dripping tragedy over soaring, epic ballads... A stunning album, Take That are the vintage champagne of pop fizzing with playful bubbles and happily maturing with age.'

'The lads have delivered a polished follow-up in remarkably quick time,' opined the *Mirror*. 'With its giddy highs and orchestral flourishes, musical glitter balls and assorted baubles, *The Circus* is skilfully stage-managed theatrical pop, which succeeds in emphasising both individual personalities and their newly established group democracy.'

'*The Circus* has pretty much got everything you'd expect from a Take That album,' said Yahoo. 'A weepy number ("Said It All"), the one aimed at inspiring you ("Julie"), the one that's romantic and lovelorn ("What Is Love") and the one that will enter the Top Ten ("Greatest Day"). As with its predecessor *Beautiful World*, *The Circus* possesses well-crafted pop songs, with faultless production. There are certainly moments when Barlow comes into his own as a songwriter. The aforementioned "Greatest Day" is a phenomenal pop ballad.'

'An album of measured, mature songwriting by all four (the quartet are all credited as writers, though Gary's recognisable hand is still the heaviest), it is by far their best,' was the view of Orange UK. 'And it isn't just a fine album; it also proves that inbetweener single "Rule the World" wasn't a one-off. Future wedding first-dance classic "Greatest Day" has a chorus capable of conjuring fireworks. Both "How Did It Come to This?" and "Hold Up a Light" are Snow Patrol-worthy stadium fillers, and the title track might just be the best (and most mournful) moment to have burst forth from Gary's piano.' Could there be any higher praise? The boys were on a roll.

CHAPTER FIFTEEN

NOTHING SUCCEEDS LIKE SUCCESS

When the tour itself finally began, it got a similarly ecstatic reception. It was an absolute spectacular, although the boys were not afraid to mock themselves. As well as coming on dressed as clowns, there was one memorable moment when Howard, Mark and Jason came on riding unicycles – while Gary rode a tricycle with training wheels. There were amazing explosions in the background, balloons took off into the sky, and dancers dressed in fat suits and cloud-covered costumes cavorted across the stage. One of the most stupendous scenes of all had the foursome atop a giant mechanical elephant: if they wanted to prove that nobody did it better, then they were successful.

'Over the coming month, close to a million people

will see Take That secure their position as Britain's most popular band with a show of such preposterous proportions and lavish excess it could make Cher sporting rhinestones seem subtle,' wrote Lisa Verrico in *The Times*. 'Like Britney Spears, Take That have themed their tour around a circus, but the boys' show makes their rival's look like an end-of-pier performance. Britney has a cast of 50? Pah, Take That have over 200. She rides an umbrella, they have a hot air balloon hovering above, but hitch a lift from the centre of the stadium to their big-top tent on a 20ft high, mechanical elephant with glowing eyes whose tail is an upside-down woman with hair extensions.'

'The atmosphere was electric and, from the onset, you could sense this was going to be a special night,' said STV. 'The magic commenced when clowns appeared in the middle of the audience blowing bubbles and riding on a mechanical cart covered in balloons, heading for a circular stage in amongst the heart of the crowd... As more and more balloons filled the centre stage, the crowd began to sense what was happening – and they were right. Suddenly Gary, Mark, Howard and Jason appeared from amongst the balloons, looking stunning in black suits.'

It had been a triumph, an absolute triumph, and the boys sensed it too. They had totally eclipsed their earlier achievements and shown themselves to be such consummate performers that they could carry on for years. Indeed, they were so pleased, they released a statement: 'To everyone who saw us on tour... Well, what can we say? We've just come to the end of some of the most incredible weeks of our lives. The tour was an even more amazing event for us than we could have possibly hoped and a very big part of that is down to the wonderful audiences we had each night. Thank you so, so much for all your continued support. We feel hugely privileged to have such brilliant fans and we hope you enjoyed the show as much as we enjoyed performing for you.'

It was safe to say the fans were pretty happy too. In September, Take That made it in to the *Guinness Book of World Records* with the fastest-selling UK tour of all time.

The charity work continued with an appearance on Children In Need Rocks the Royal Albert Hall. This, too, had been organised by Gary, who had clearly developed something of a social conscience, and someone else was there that night, too. 'What a perfect night for us to introduce an old friend,' said Gary, and there he was, the Robster himself, singing from his new album, two numbers called 'Bodies' and 'You Know Me'. The warmth and affection between the two men were such that, after 15 years, it was clear a reunion really was on the cards now.

Robbie himself appeared to be deeply moved. 'I started tearing up just before I came on,' he said, 'and the lads were singing and knowing it was just about to happen and knowing what the reactions were going to be like. And then all my team were like, "Please don't cry." I think we should have milked it for a lot longer than we actually did. I think Gaz, in his wisdom, went, "Right, we should get off now – let the lad do his singing." I was trying to get them back to do a bow and everything. That's the first time in fifteen years: we should have at least stayed there for ten minutes.' By this time, Robbie clearly wanted them as much as – if not more than – they wanted him. At long last, it was finally going to happen.

The whole event was a triumph and reflected very well on Gary, who now had the clout to pull this kind of thing together. Other performers included Sir Paul McCartney – with whom Take That sang 'Hey Jude', Dame Shirley Bassey, Annie Lennox, Cheryl Cole, Dizzee Rascal, Sir Terry Wogan, Lily Allen, Leona Lewis and many more. Nor did it escape anyone's notice that, by the end of the show, Robbie and Gary were standing side by side. It was a remarkable evening all round and one that was rewarded when

Gary was presented with a *Blue Peter* gold badge, for outstanding achievements and inspiring children. Other recipients, and there weren't very many of them, included Lenny Henry, Jenson Button and HM the Queen.

It was time for another release: *Take That Present The Circus Live*. Another record was broken: it became the fastest selling DVD in the UK, smashing previous records in one day. The boys shifted 82,414 copies in just 24 hours, giving them their 4th consecutive UK No 1 DVD, and smashing their own record for the *Beautiful World Live* DVD, which had shifted 64,000 copies in its 1st week and had, until then, been the fastest-selling DVD in the UK.

In early 2010, the emphasis on both professional and charity work continued. The boys agreed to sing on a charity single to help victims of the dreadful earthquake in Haiti and, although he didn't sing with them, Robbie contributed to the single from LA. Awards continued to pile up, with Take That winning Best Group at the Virgin Media Awards, while Mark walked away with Hottest Male.

More to the point, they were happy. 'The dynamic within the band now is completely different,' said Mark in an early interview after they got back together. 'We make the effort to talk. I think we can turn to each other now. We've got more in common and I think there's a lot more soul in us now. None of us saw it coming. I don't think we even wanted it. It's not like one of us has been calling the others for years, saying, "Let's get back together." It was never going to happen. And now it's happening.'

It was at this point, however, that the various scandals mentioned earlier came to light. While they did nothing to dent the boys' popularity, there was still a slight sense of shock that anyone in Take That – above all, Mark – should have been caught up in such a mess. It was certainly ironic, given that Mr Scandal himself, Robbie, had cleaned up his own act so comprehensively. His career was not what it had been, though. If ever there was a time for old bandmates to come together and heal old wounds, that time was now.

Everyone involved was very concerned to make it clear that there was no bad blood between them whatsoever. Gary and Robbie gave their first joint interview for 15 years, to Chris Moyles, and tackled the subject head on. Robbie started by talking about their recent meeting in LA. 'I was very nervous because there were four of them,' he said. 'I came so close to not going because I had toothache that night and I'd just taken a painkiller. I was quite large as well and I thought, "I can't go mumbling, looking like Elvis." I'd said some nasty things about Gaz. What do I do if I go in? Is he harbouring anything? So the missus pushed me through the door. It was very exciting, very liberating.'

After that, he invited the band back to his house the next night, where he was able to talk openly to Gary. 'I spent the last fifteen years thinking what I was going to say,' he said. 'We had that big chat and the most amazing thing happened at the end of it – we both said "sorry" to each other and we both meant it. That's all we needed. It just lifted so much off my shoulders that I didn't know was still there. It was the start of a very magical eighteen months that we've had since then, writing songs together, getting to know each other. It's nice being able to be grown-ups and hear each other and say "sorry" because not many people can do that.'

The reconciliation was also a huge relief to Gary. 'All these things had been built up for so long, they just sounded stupid as they were coming out,' he said. 'We just needed to sit opposite each other and talk. I must say, I had a good sleep after that.'

'You've got to be ready to take some responsibility for your own actions, as well,' added Robbie. 'And fortunately, we were both in a place to go, "Yeah, that happened, that wasn't too great. I'm not proud of it and I'm sorry." It's so many rehabs ago. There's so much vodka underneath the bridge.'

Indeed, there were regrets all round. The rest of Take That had also accepted that they could have done more to help – Robbie was, after all, awfully young when he joined them. 'I think we had a lot of guilt, the four of us, because Rob was the youngest, the most impressionable of all of us,' said Gary. 'We always felt like we didn't look after him enough. If there was one big thing we sat and regretted, it was always that.' It was something that everyone needed to hear.

When Gary and Robbie did finally start work together, no one, given Robbie's history of making teasing remarks about being gay, should have been surprised at what ensued. The two recorded a single, 'Shame', but the accompanying video bore clear references to *Brokeback Mountain*, the cowboy movie about cowboys who were also in love. In the video – full of sly glances at each other – they first encounter each other when shopping (it could hardly have got more arch), before going off for a drink in a bar. Much smouldering ensues. The two then head off for a remote part of a river, where they strip off their tops – after his strict diet and exercise regime, Gary could hold his own with Robbie – and head into the rocks. The twist is that they are actually stripping off to dive into the river, which, after an attack of nerves, they then fail to do.

It was pure Robbie, if not so much Gary, but the two played it dead straight and poked fun at their 'bromance'. 'It was amazing, not awkward at all,' said Robbie. 'I love Gary to bits. Ayda calls him my boyfriend.' What Dawn called Robbie was not revealed, but the good-humoured aspect to it all was plain to see.

So what of the future? The reunion that everyone has been waiting for – well, almost everyone; some fans of the foursome have expressed doubts – was finally going to happen. But whether it will be any more than a one-off is open to question. 'I don't know the answer to that,' said Gary. 'We agreed when we started – it's twenty years since we began, it's our twentieth year for all of us – to do a one-off album and maybe a one-off tour would be a great thing this year. But I think, once we've done that, Rob will go back to being Rob, we'll go back to being a four. I think it will resume to how it was.'

Robbie was also careful to keep his options open. 'The thing is, the door is open to do whatever we want,' he said. 'We've got eighteen months planned.

Whatever happens after, happens after that. We haven't decided.'

'We are talking about a tour right now, so hopefully next summer, we will tour,' said Gary.

'There's some stuff on the cards but there's only so much we can talk about now,' added Robbie. 'There's big plans in the works but when, where and what, we're not allowed to say. Plus, we don't really know.'

And that was that. In many ways, it was the best possible outcome: 20 years after the group had formed, they were all at peace with one another once more. They had defied all expectations about their longevity and staying power, and it is barely accurate to call them a boy band any more (and not just because they're all in their late 30s and early 40s). Take That no longer just have a teen fan base: it stretches across generations now. They have gone far beyond just teen idols to all-round and much-loved entertainers. More than one has conquered his own demons, but the band got through it all and showed that they could still put on a show like no one else.

Above all, though, theirs is a story of making peace, of laying bitterness to rest, of second chances and of friendship. It will be no surprise if, 20 years from now, Take That is still going strong.